I cannot overexaggerate how good this book is. Here is a crash course in life-changing biblical teaching, a wake up call to the slumbering, a blood transfusion for the spiritually anemic, a solid meal for the mature—and much more: conversational, cutting where needed, gospel-filled—and clear.

The Good News We Almost Forgot has it all: honesty, truth, grace, plain-speaking, encouragement, wisdom, and hope. It may not make you wish you were Dutch—but it should certainly make you feel that being a Christian is the greatest thing in the world, today or any day!

    —SINCLAIR B FERGUSON
        Senior Minister, First Presbyterian Church, Columbia, SC

I'm sure this will be the best book on the Heidelberg Catechism I've ever read. I know it will be the first.

    —C. J. MAHANEY
        President, Sovereign Grace Ministries

For more than four centuries, reformed Christians have gleaned rich biblical insights and found immense comfort from the Heidelberg Catechism (1563). Kevin DeYoung's concise commentary on this beloved confession is excellent, full of wisdom and relevance for contemporary Christians. Here the reader will find nothing less than a celebration of the beauty of Christ and the glory of the gospel.

    —SCOTT M. MANETSCH
        Associate Professor of Church History and Christian Thought
        Trinity Evangelical Divinity School

When I was a teenager, Tuesday nights were catechism nights. I would go to church and, under the tutelage of the pastor, both study and memorize what I affectionately called "Ye Olde Heidelberger." The deep truths of that document provided a firm foundation for my growing faith. Even as a teen I realized that at the very heart of the Heidelberg Catechism is the gospel of Jesus Christ. And yet I cannot deny that it has been many years since I last studied it. In *The Good News We Almost Forgot* Kevin DeYoung dusts off that old catechism and proves that it is as relevant today as it was 450 years ago. Its truths are timeless, its encouragement unchanged. I am grateful to Kevin for introducing this venerable document to a new generation of believers. May they find hope and joy in the One it celebrates.

    —TIM CHALLIES

W9-BNK-493

As Kevin DeYoung writes, "The gospel summarized in the Heidelberg Catechism is glorious." I could not agree more. And it is my prayer that DeYoung's often whimsical, always insightful, and invariably accessible reflections on the catechism will help many to catch a greater glimpse of that glorious gospel.

—GARY PARRETT
    Professor of Educational Ministries and Worship
    Gordon-Conwell Theological Seminary

The Heidelberg Catechism is one of the most important documents to emerge from the Reformation. In the space of one hundred twenty-nine questions and answers it captures a vital Christian theology, piety, and practice. Christians and congregations alike will benefit greatly from getting to know this classic resource and we shall all be thankful for Kevin DeYoung's wonderfully accessible introduction to this resource.

—R. SCOTT CLARK, DPhil
    Professor of Church History and Historical Theology
    Westminster Seminary California

De Young has brought an old catechism to new life. This book is a wonderfully clear and contemporary introduction and explanation of the Heidelberg Catechism. It is interesting, well illustrated, and biblically based. I plan to recommend it to those new to the Catechism and those who want a fresh read through it. It is a gift to today's church.

—THOMAS GROELSEMA
    Senior Pastor, 1st Byron Center CRC

The

GOOD NEWS
WE ALMOST
FORGOT

REDISCOVERING *the* GOSPEL
in a 16th CENTURY CATECHISM

KEVIN L. DeYOUNG

MOODY PUBLISHERS
CHICAGO

The edition of the Heidelberg Catechism used throughout this book is reprinted from
Ecumenical Creeds and Reformed Confessions © 1988 Faith Alive Christian Resources
http://www.faithaliveresources.org.

All Scripture quotations, unless otherwise indicated, are taken from *The Holy Bible,
English Standard Version.* Copyright © 2000, 2001 by Crossway Bibles, a division of
Good News Publishers. Used by permission. All rights reserved.
Scripture quotations marked KJV are taken from the King James Version.
Scripture quotations marked NIV are taken from the *Holy Bible, New International
Version*®. NIV®. Copyright © 1973, 1978, 1984 by Biblica, Inc.™ Used by permission of
Zondervan. All rights reserved.
Scripture quotations marked NRSV are from the *New Revised Standard Version* of the
Bible, copyright 1989, by the Division of Christian Education of the National Council
of the Churches of Christ in the USA. Used by permission. All rights reserved.

Editor: Jim Vincent
Interior Design: Ragont Design   Cover Design: Studio Gearbox
Author Photo: LCH Photography   Cover Image: www.photos.com

Library of Congress Cataloging-in-Publication Data

DeYoung, Kevin.
   The good news we almost forgot : rediscovering the Gospel in a 16th
century catechism / Kevin L. DeYoung.
     p. cm.
   Includes bibliographical references.
   ISBN 978-0-8024-5840-7
   1. Heidelberger Katechismus. 2. Reformed Church--Catechisms. I. Title.
BX9428.D49 2010
238'.42--dc22
                                                              2009053552

To Ian, Jacob, Elsie, and Paul.

Daddy loves you more than you know.

I hope you grow up to like the Heidelberg Catechism

half as much as I do.

Contents

Foreword

*E*veryone is a theologian, like it or not. The atheist who says, "There is no God" is a theologian of sorts. His theology is that the God of the Bible does not exist. For the Christian, the atheist is easy to peg. We know hands down that his theology is bad. We are not likely to be deceived by him.

But what about the Christian who says something like, "My God is a God of love," meaning God wouldn't send anyone to hell? That's also bad theology, but not as easy to spot as that of the atheist. The problem is, it's partly true. God *is* a God of love. In fact, the Bible says, "God is love" (1 John 4:8). Love is not an add-on to God's character. It is part of His essential nature.

So what's wrong with the statement, "My God is a God of love"? First are the words "my God." "My God" is the product of one's own personal belief of what he or she thinks God is like. It is not based on any external, objective information.

The second error in "my God is a God of love" is that it ignores the fact that God is also a God of justice and righteousness. It ignores the fact that the Bible says, "For the wrath of God is revealed from heaven against all ungodliness and unrighteousness of men" (Romans 1:18). Because it ignores the bad news of God's righteous judgment, it fails to tell us the really good news that the God of love did indeed love us so much that He sent His Son to die for our sins (1 John 4:10, 1 Corinthians 15:1–3).

This is just one illustration of the bad theology abroad among Christians today. There are others. There is the theology that denies the divine inspiration and consequent authority of Scripture. There is the theology that denies or downplays the substitutionary death of Christ for our sins. There is the theology that belittles the importance or relevance of the local church. There's a lot of bad theology among us today because Christians are not getting their theology from the Bible. That's where *The Good News We Almost Forgot*, by Kevin DeYoung, can help us. This book is based squarely on the Bible. It can help make us Bible-based theologians. How is this so?

Well, Pastor DeYoung's book is about a catechism, and a sixteenth-century catechism at that. I suspect some Christians today might ask, "What's a catechism?" For many others, catechism might sound like something out of grandma's attic; old and dusty, and hopelessly out-of-date. And for a large group of Christians today a catechism seems like a man-made add-on to the Bible.

Some responses: A catechism is simply a means of instruction by posting a series of questions about God and humankind, and answering those questions from the Bible. A catechism is never out-of-date as it seeks to teach us the eternal truths of Scripture. And a catechism is not a man-made add-on to the Bible; it's instruction in good theology derived from the Scriptures. None of us are smart enough or spiritual enough to dig out various truths of Scripture by ourselves. We need sound instruction, and a good catechism provides that.

I've said that Pastor DeYoung's book is about a catechism. More specifically it is about the Heidelberg Catechism, written by a team of theology professors and pastors, and first published in Heidelberg, Germany, in 1563. I'll leave it to pastor DeYoung to expand further on this in his excellent introduction to this book.

I myself belong to a church that uses a different catechism, but for many years I have been an admirer of, and have profited from the Heidelberg Catechism. I like its structure which, as pastor DeYoung points out, fits into the pattern of salvation found in the book of Romans; namely *guilt*, *grace*, and *gratitude*. It is the same pattern so clearly seen in Isaiah's vision of the holiness of God in the temple (Isaiah 6:1–8). In fact I would say that these words form the overall storyline of the Bible.

I believe this sequence of words, or better, concepts, is the only proper way to understand and apply the Bible to our lives. Yet my perception of the Christian community today is that we are largely imperative driven. We major on the "ought to" and "how to" with little regard for that which makes us "want to." But the Bible does not do this. Considering its overall message, it teaches us that our obedience to the moral imperatives of the Bible should be a response of gratitude more than of duty. Not that duty is wrong. It's just that God wants us to delight to do that which is our duty to do. And that which makes us delight to obey and serve God is gratitude for his grace shown to us in the gospel of Jesus Christ.

Strange as it may seem, Christians need the gospel as much as unbelievers do. We do not need the gospel to "be saved." We need the gospel to keep us from lapsing into a performance mind-set in our day-to-day relationship with God. We need the gospel to remind us that we are still practicing sinners whose only hope for both eternal life and today's blessings from God are "Jesus' blood and righteousness."

The *Heidelberg Catechism*, rightly reflected on, will help us keep the concepts of our guilt, God's grace, and our response of gratitude in the correct sequence in our lives. And Kevin DeYoung does a masterful job of showing us what each of these three concepts look like in everyday life.

Pastor DeYoung is a minister in the Reformed Church of America, a denomination with roots in the Dutch Reformed Church, and he writes from the perspective of this historic confessional tradition. Consequently there will be a few points in this book that readers from a non-Reformed position will disagree with. But don't be put off by these few points of disagreement. Overall this is an exciting book that will prove helpful to people of all theological persuasions. I commend it to you as a book that will help all of us be better Bible-based theologians.

JERRY BRIDGES
Author of *The Pursuit of Holiness*

Introduction:
Hide-and-Seek
and the Heidelberg

The only thing more difficult than finding the truth is not losing it. What starts out as new and precious becomes plain and old. What begins a thrilling discovery becomes a rote exercise. What provokes one generation to sacrifice and passion becomes in the next generation a cause for rebellion and apathy. Why is it that denominations and church movements almost always drift from their theological moorings? Why is it that people who grow up in the church are often less articulate about their faith than the new Christian who converted at forty-five? Why is it that those who grow up with creeds and confessions are usually the ones who hate them most?

Perhaps it's because truth is like the tip of your nose—it's hardest to see when it's right in front of you.

No doubt, the church in the West has many new things to learn. But for the most part, everything we need to learn is what we've already forgotten. The chief theological task now facing the Western church is not to reinvent or to be relevant but to remember. We must remember the old, old story. We must remember the faith once delivered to the saints. We must remember the truths that spark reformation, revival, and regeneration.

And because we want to remember all this, we must also remember—if we are fortunate enough to have ever heard of them in the first place—our creeds, confessions, and catechisms.

Your reaction to that last sentence probably falls in one of three categories. Some people, especially the young, believe it or not, will think, "Cool. Ancient faith. I'm into creeds and confessions." Others will think, "Wait a minute, don't Catholics have catechisms? Why do we need some man-made document to tell us what to think? I have no creed but the Bible, thank you very much." And yet others—the hardest soil of all—want nothing more than to be done with all this catechism business. "Been there, done that. *Bor*-ing. I've seen people who knew their creeds backward and forward and didn't make them missional, passionate, or even very nice."

To all three groups I simply say, "Come and see." Come and see what vintage faith is really all about. Come and see if the cool breeze from centuries gone by can awaken your lumbering faith. Come and see if your church was lame *because* of its confessions and catechisms or if your lame church *made* the confessions and catechisms lame all on its own. Whether you've grown up with confessions and catechisms or they sound like something from another spiritual planet, I say, "Come and see." Come and see Christ in the unlikeliest of places—in a manger, in Nazareth, or even in Heidelberg.

BETTER THAN YOU MIGHT THINK
(Not as Bad as You Remember)

I love the Heidelberg Catechism, not like I love my wife or I love the Bible, but in a deeper way than I love the Chicago Bears and a more eternal way than I love a good deep-dish pizza. "Love" and "Catechism" are not two words usually heard together, unless it's something like "I love that my church doesn't make kids learn catechism anymore." Nevertheless, I freely confess I love the Heidelberg Catechism. I love it because it's old, it's biblical, and it's true. It's not perfect. It's not infallible. It says too little about some subjects and too much about some others. But it is through and through trustworthy and beautiful, simple and deep. Most of all, I love the Heidelberg Catechism because I love the gospel it expounds and the salvation it proclaims.

I grew up with the Heidelberg. I don't recall having to memorize it cold like some organic chemistry nightmare. It wasn't front and center in my life, but it was there. I'll forever be grateful to my childhood pastor for making me read the Heidelberg Catechism and meet in his office with him to talk about it before I made a profession of faith in the fourth grade. I was nervous to meet with him, even more nervous to meet before all the elders. But both meetings were pleasant. And besides, I was forced to read through all 129 questions and answers at age nine. That was a blessing I didn't realize at the time. Ever since then I've had a copy of the Catechism and have grown to understand it and cherish it more and more over the years.

Not everyone is as keen on catechism as I am. For some, catechisms are too linear, too systematic, too propositional. For others, the catechism gets a bad rap because, fairly or unfairly, the only stories that we hear about catechetical instruction are the stories of old Domine VanderSo-and-so who threatened to smite us hip and thigh if we couldn't remember what God required of us in the Eighth Commandment. More often, catechisms simply never get tried because they are said to be about theology, and theology is said to be boring . . . and words like "Heidelberg" and "Westminster" are even more boring. (Incidentally, I have never been a fan of snazzy Sunday school curriculum that tries to pretend that a catechism is something other than questions and answers about the Bible. You can call it "Journeys with God from the Palatinate" or "Heidelberg Truth Rockets" but it's still a catechism, and our kids know it.)

But even with all this bad press, I think the Catechism can make a comeback. All of us—kids and adults—need to know the Bible better than we know the Heidelberg Catechism. No doubt about that. But all of us—kids and adults—can have our faith strengthened, our knowledge broadened, and our love for Jesus deepened by devoting ourselves to reading rich truth like the kind found in the Heidelberg Catechism. I'll never forget sitting in my Christian education class at my evangelical, non-Dutch, nondenominational seminary. One of our assigned texts was the Heidelberg Catechism—this little book that growing up was usually good for rolling the eyes of students into the backs of their little heads. But my fellow students at seminary marveled at this piece of work. "Where has this been all our lives?" "This will be perfect for Sunday school!" "I'm going to use this for new members' classes!" Most of the Dutch Reformed kids I knew were ready to see the Heidelberg Catechism go the way of the dodo bird. But at seminary, my classmates were seeing something many of my peers had missed. The Heidelberg Catechism is really, really good.

PURPOSE-DRIVEN TRUTH

In 1562, Elector Frederick III of the Palatinate, a princely state of the Holy Roman Empire (think Germany), ordered the preparation of a new catechism for his territory. A new catechism would serve three purposes: (1) as a tool for teaching children, (2) as a guide for preachers, and (3) as a form for confessional unity among the Protestant factions in the Palatinate. Frederick wanted a unifying catechism that avoided theological labels and was plainly rooted in the texts of Scripture. To that end, he commissioned a team of theological professors and ministers (along with Frederick himself) to draft a new catechism. Although the catechism was truly a team effort (including Caspar Olevianus who used to be considered a coauthor of the catechism, but now is seen as simply one valuable member of the committee), there is little doubt the chief author was Zacharias Ursinus.

Ursinus, a professor at the University in Heidelberg, was born on July 18, 1534, in what is today Poland but at that time was part of Austria. Ursinus was the chief architect of the Heidelberg Catechism, basing many of the questions and answers on his own shorter catechism, and to a lesser extent, his larger catechism. The Heidelberg Catechism reflects Ursinus's theological convictions (firmly Protestant with Calvinist leanings) and his warm, irenic spirit.[1]

This new catechism was first published in Heidelberg (the leading city of the Palatinate) in January 1563, going through several revisions that same year. The Catechism was quickly translated into Latin and Dutch, and soon after into French and English. Besides the Bible, John Bunyan's *Pilgrim's Progress*, and Thomas à Kempis' *Imitation of Christ*, the Heidelberg Catechism is the most widely circulated book in the world. Since its publication in 1563, the Heidelberg Catechism has been used in scores of languages and is widely praised as the most devotional, most loved catechism of the Reformation.[2]

Like most catechisms, the Heidelberg Catechism is largely a

commentary on three things: the Apostle's Creed, the Ten Commandments, and the Lord's Prayer. Heidelberg's structure, however, is unique in two ways. First, the overall structure fits into the pattern of salvation found in the book of Romans. After two introductory questions, the Catechism deals with man's misery (Questions 3–11), man's deliverance (12–85), and finally, man's response (86–129)—or to put it more memorably: guilt, grace, and gratitude. Second, the Heidelberg Catechism's 129 questions and answers are divided into fifty-two Lord's Days. Besides making it easy to preach from the Catechism (one of its original purposes), this division also makes the Catechism convenient for family devotions every Sunday or personal catechetical reflection once a week.

YEAR OF THE HEIDELBERG

Not too long ago I devoted an entire year to studying the Heidelberg Catechism. In lieu of my usual monthly church newsletter, I decided to try weekly devotions on the Heidelberg Catechism. Jesus' words about counting the cost came to mind more than once before launching such an undertaking. Would I really make the time—at least three hours a week—to jot down my musings on a 450-year-old catechism? And would anybody read them if I did? I mean, Heidelberg's good, but it's not exactly *Lord of the Rings*. In the end, I'm convinced it was a good undertaking, worth the time and commitment. More seemed to read the devotionals than I thought, and some dear saints made their own binders and faithfully picked up their Lord's Day reading every week in the lobby.

Just as importantly, the Heidelberg Catechism has been good for me. My own personal assessment of my pastoral ministry is that over the past two or three years the gospel has become much more central. Not that I didn't know the gospel or didn't believe or preach the gospel before. But recently, I have taken more delight in the gospel, stayed more focused on the gospel, and made the gospel more explicit in my ministry. The Heidelberg Catechism is partly to thank for this renewed passion. In a church age confused about the essential elements of the Christian faith—and whether Christianity has any doctrinal center at all—the Heidelberg Catechism offers a relentless reminder of the one doctrine that matters most:

We are great sinners and Christ is a greater Savior. I wouldn't have spent a year in the Catechism if I didn't think that doing so would help me know the Bible better and love Jesus more. Mercifully, I believe my year of the Heidelberg did just that.

Those cheery thoughts notwithstanding, I must add that I am saddened to think of how many Christians—Protestants, evangelicals, and Reformed Christians in particular—are blissfully unaware of this treasure right under their noses. I am even more disappointed to think of pastors and professors in the Reformed tradition (and here I'm thinking of mushy mainliners and atheological practitioners) who have been instructed in the Catechism and simply don't cherish the truths it proclaims.

But I'm also optimistic to think how the Spirit might work if a new generation of children, students, pastors, and regular Christian folk thrilled to the gospel so elegantly and logically laid out in the Heidelberg Catechism. The Heidelberg Catechism is simple enough for children and new believers and for anyone who wants a better grounding for his faith. It's also deep enough to pull longtime Christians past the sentimental platitudes and "deeds not creeds" neoliberalism that passes for evangelical spirituality and into cleaner, healthier waters. I daresay the Catechism can even be used evangelistically as a clearheaded, warmhearted explanation of the Christian faith.

A LABOR OF LOVE

I have been privileged to have a few books published before this one. And while I loved working on all of them and trust they all were of some help to the church, none of them warmed my soul and drew me closer to God like this one. This book may not seem as timely and I doubt royalty sales will cause me to seek out tax-sheltered annuities, but that's not why Christians should write books anyway. I wrote this book so that others might be drawn into the same gospel ocean that has refreshed me. The gospel summarized in the Heidelberg Catechism is glorious, its Christ gracious, its comfort rich, its Spirit strong, its God sovereign, and its truth timeless. You can meet Christ here, if you will simply come and see.

If you've ever found understanding the Bible a bit like exploring America on foot, interesting but overwhelming and slow-going, why not use the Heidelberg Catechism as a map? The Catechism can help show you the main attractions others have discovered in the Bible and lead you to the best, most important truths of our faith.[3] As the saying goes (to change our metaphors once again), you can see farther when standing on the shoulders of giants. And the Heidelberg Catechism is a giant of mind-sharpening, Christ-worshiping, soul-inspiring devotion. Stand on its shoulders and see more of Christ who saves us from our guilt by His grace and makes us, through His Spirit, wholeheartedly willing and ready to live for Him.

$\mathcal{L}$ord's Day 1

1. Q. WHAT IS YOUR ONLY COMFORT IN LIFE AND IN
   DEATH?[4]

   A. That I am not my own, but belong—body and soul, in life and in
   death—to my faithful Savior Jesus Christ. He has fully paid for all
   my sins with His precious blood, and has set me free from the
   tyranny of the devil. He also watches over me in such a way that
   not a hair can fall from my head without the will of my Father in
   heaven: in fact, all things must work together for my salvation.
   Because I belong to Him, Christ, by His Holy Spirit, assures me of
   eternal life and makes me wholeheartedly willing and ready from
   now on to live for Him.

2. Q. WHAT MUST YOU KNOW TO LIVE AND DIE IN THE JOY
   OF THIS COMFORT?

   A. Three things: first, how great my sin and misery are; second, how
   I am set free from all my sins and misery; third, how I am to thank
   God for such deliverance.

Comfort,
Comfort My People,
Says Your God

The first question is easily the most famous in the Catechism. It may be the only part of the Catechism most Christians (even Reformed ones) ever hear. But I suppose, if you get to hear just one, this is a pretty good one to get.

The only catechism question as well known as this one is the first question of the Westminster Shorter Catechism: "What is the chief end of man? To glorify God and enjoy him forever." I've heard the Heidelberg criticized for beginning with man (what is *my* only comfort) instead of beginning with the glory of God like Westminster. But if we want to be picky, Westminster can be criticized for starting with what we ought to do rather than with what Christ has done for us, like the Heidelberg.

In truth, both catechisms start in appropriate places. Heidelberg starts with grace. Westminster starts with glory. We'd be hard-pressed to think of two better words to describe the theme of biblical revelation.

Heidelberg's first question is so striking because of the word "only." If it asked "what comforts" you, that would be a polite but underwhelming question. I'm comforted by sleep, chocolate chip cookies, a good book, and the soundtrack from *The Mission*. But when the Catechism asks what is your *only* comfort, it is getting at something deeper. "Comfort" translates the German word *trost*, which was, in turn, rendered *consolatio* in the first official Latin version. *Trost* is related to the

English word "trust" and has the root meaning of "certainty" or "protection." Heidelberg is asking, "What is your solace in life? What is your only real security?"

Heidelberg's first question not only sets the theme for the whole Catechism (see Q/A 2, 52, 53, 57, 58), it also poses the most important question we will ever face. What enables you to endure life and face death unafraid? Is it that you read your Bible every day? That you attend church every Sunday? That you give to the poor? That you have a cushy retirement account saved up? That you haven't committed any of the big sins in life?

We live in a world where we expect to find comfort in possessions, pride, power, and position. But the Catechism teaches us that our only true comfort comes from the fact that we don't even belong to ourselves. How countercultural and counterintuitive! We can endure suffering and disappointment in life and face death and the life to come without fear of judgment, not because of what we've done or what we own or who we are, but because of what we do not possess, namely, our own selves.

Heidelberg's emphasis on belonging to Christ probably comes from John Calvin. Some people have the impression that John Calvin was a rigid, arid dogmatician, but actually his was a profoundly God-entranced heart. Listen to the passionate beat of Calvin's heart in this passage, which finds an echo in the Heidelberg Catechism: "We are not our own: let not our reason nor our will, therefore, sway our plans and deeds. We are not our own: let us therefore not set it as our goal to seek what is expedient for us according to the flesh. We are not our own: in so far as we can, let us therefore forget ourselves and all that is ours. Conversely, we are God's: let us therefore live for him and die for him. We are God's: let his wisdom and will therefore rule all our actions. We are God's: let all the parts of our life accordingly strive toward him as our only lawful goal."[5]

Question 1 of the Catechism shapes our whole existence. The first thing we need to know as a Christian is that we belong to Jesus and not ourselves.

But it doesn't help much to know all about comfort and joy if we don't know what is required to live and die in this comfort and joy. Belonging to Jesus and not ourselves means knowing three things: *guilt, grace,* and *gratitude.* The rest of the Catechism will follow this threefold outline.

First, we understand our sin. Then we understand salvation. And finally we understand how we are sanctified to serve.

All three things are necessary. If we don't know about our sin—which brings a true sense of guilt—we will be too confident in our abilities to do right and make the world a better place. We will ignore our most fundamental problem, which is not lack of education, or lack of opportunity, or lack of resources but sin and its attendant misery. But if we don't know how we are set free from this sin and misery—which comes through God's grace—we will try to fix ourselves in futility or give up altogether in despair. And if we don't know how to thank God, showing gratitude for such deliverance, we will live in a self-centered, self-referential bubble, which is not why God saved us from our sin and misery in the first place. If Christians would hold to all "three things" and not just one or two, we would be saved from a lot of poor theology and bad ideas.

And don't miss the underlying assumption in these first two questions: we are *meant* to live and die in the joy of this comfort. That so few Christians do is a testimony to both how hard life can be and how little we meditate on what it means to belong to Christ. Comfort does not mean Christ makes all the bad things in life go away. Comfort, as Ursinus put it, "results from a certain process of reasoning, in which we oppose something good to something evil, that by a proper consideration of this good, we may mitigate our grief, and patiently endure the evil."[6] In other words, comfort puts before us a greater joy to outweigh present and anticipated sufferings.

When we think of living and dying in comfort, we imagine La-Z-Boy recliners, back rubs, and all the food you can eat (with none of the pounds, of course). But the Catechism has in mind a different kind of comfort, one that is deeper, higher, richer, and sweeter. We find this comfort by admitting our sin, instead of excusing it; by trusting in Another instead of ourselves; and by living to give thanks instead of being thanked.

*L*ord's Day 2

3. Q. HOW DO YOU COME TO KNOW YOUR MISERY?

A. The law of God tells me.

4. Q. WHAT DOES GOD'S LAW REQUIRE OF US?

A. Christ teaches us this in summary in Matthew 22—"Love the Lord your God with all your heart and with all your soul and with all your mind and with all your strength. This is the first and greatest commandment. And the second is like it: Love your neighbor as yourself. All the Law and the Prophets hang on these two commandments."

5. Q. CAN YOU LIVE UP TO ALL THIS PERFECTLY?

A. No. I have a natural tendency to hate God and my neighbor.

Misery Loves Company

*C*ompared with the amount of time spent on other topics, the Heidelberg Catechism does not spend a lot of time on human depravity. The grace section of the Catechism covers twenty-seven Lord's Days and seventy-four Questions and Answers. The gratitude section is only a little shorter, covering twenty-one Lord's Days and forty-four Questions and Answers. The guilt section is by far the shortest with only three Lord's Days and nine Questions and Answers. The authors of the Catechism wanted Heidelberg to be an instrument of comfort, not condemnation.

But they also realized that true, lasting consolation can only come to those who know of their need to be consoled. The first thing we need in order to experience the comfort of the gospel is to be made uncomfortable with our sin. The comfort of the gospel doesn't skirt around the issue of sin, or ignore it like positive thinking preachers and self-help gurus. It looks at sin square in the eye, acknowledges it, and deals with it. While many people will tell us to stop focusing on sin and to lighten up because we aren't "bad" people, the Catechism tells us just the opposite. In order to have comfort, we must first see our sin-induced misery.

And the way we see our misery is through the law. The law is good (1 Tim. 1:8), so the problem is not with the law per se. The problem is that we cannot keep the law. Any careful, protracted meditation on the Ten Commandments, let alone the 613 commandments of the Torah, will leave the honest person feeling rather like Eeyore—gloomy, gray, and depressed. The Bible is full of many wonderful ethical commands, which would be very inspiring except for the fact that we are not wonderful, ethical people.

We often hear that all religions are basically the same in that they all encourage us to love our neighbors, help the poor, forgive others, and generally be kind, compassionate people. Even if this were true (which it isn't when you get down to specifics), it would miss the point, because Christianity is not a religion mainly about a moral code to keep. Christianity is about a God who saves people who don't keep the moral code.

The law doesn't inspire me to be a better me or find the god within me. The law beats me down and shows me how miserable I am. In all the fussing over the Ten Commandments in courthouses and school buildings in this country, have we forgotten that the law is more than a great set of principles? Yes, the law has a lot of great principles, and all of them are intended to show us how great we are not.

But let's be clear: Jesus believed in the law. He did not come to abolish it (Matt. 5:17). Jesus wants us to love God and love our neighbor as the fulfillment of all the Old Testament rules and regulations. That's why Jesus taught this simple and beautiful summary of the law as recorded in Matthew 22.

But Jesus' standard is unattainable. I often hear the gospel (mis)explained nowadays as merely an invitation into a kingdom way of life. It's said, for example, that Jesus' statement in John 14:6 about being the way, the truth, and the life simply means, to some, that Jesus is the best way to live. It is certainly true that Jesus is the best way to live, but no one lives like Jesus! We never have and we never will.

We don't live like Jesus because without the Spirit's work in our lives, we can't. Most of us can't keep our houses clean like we want, or stick to a budget like we desire, or manage our time like we mean to. So what makes us think we can live like Jesus and do everything a holy God requires of us? The Catechism puts the matter rather bluntly: "I have a natural tendency to hate God and my neighbor." That sentence sums up a gigabyte of biblical teaching. No one is righteous (Rom. 3:10). All have sinned and fall short of the glory of God (Rom. 3:23). The human heart is deceitful above all things, and desperately sick (Jer. 17:9). The natural man is dead in trespasses and sin (Eph. 2:1). By nature, we pass our days in malice and envy, hated by others and hating one another (Titus 3:3). The passages just keep coming, pounding us into submission until we cry "Holy, holy, holy is the Lord of hosts. . . . Woe is me! For I am lost . . ." (Isa. 6:3, 5).

We can't keep 613 commandments perfectly. Neither can we keep ten. We can't even keep two. Isn't it ironic that the Catechism shows us our misery through one of the most treasured, devotional passages in all the Scriptures? Everyone loves Matthew 22. "Just teach the two great commandments," people say. "Avoid theological wrangling. Avoid doctrine and propositions. Love God; love neighbor—this is what it means to follow Jesus." True enough, but where do we turn for comfort when we despised God and ignored our neighbor for the tenth time today? Do you really love God with every fiber of your being, never putting any person or dream or possession before Him? And do you really love your neighbor as yourself, always aiming for the advancement of others, always putting the needs of others ahead of your own, and always treating others just as you wish to be treated?

Many people, well-meaning church leaders included, are eager to boil down Christianity to the great commandments, or the Sermon on the Mount, or the Beatitudes, or Micah 6:8, or some other powerful summary of God's ethical intentions. But if all I have are God's ethical intentions for my life, I'm in a worse fix than simply losing my tail like Eeyore. My own efforts to be a good person are, in comparison to what God requires of me, positively miserable. I'll be damned, discouraged, and dismayed if being a follower of Jesus means nothing but a new set of things I'm supposed to do for Him. Instead, my following Jesus should be, first of all, a declaration of all that He has done for me.

6. Q. DID GOD CREATE PEOPLE SO WICKED AND PERVERSE?

A. No. God created them good and in His own image, that is, in true righteousness and holiness, so that they might truly know God their creator, love Him with all their heart, and live with Him in eternal happiness for His praise and glory.

7. Q. THEN WHERE DOES THIS CORRUPT HUMAN NATURE COME FROM?

A. From the fall and disobedience of our first parents, Adam and Eve, in Paradise. This fall has so poisoned our nature that we are born sinners—corrupt from conception on.

8. Q. BUT ARE WE SO CORRUPT THAT WE ARE TOTALLY UNABLE TO DO ANY GOOD AND INCLINED TOWARD ALL EVIL?

A. Yes, unless we are born again, by the Spirit of God.

It's Really That Bad

*W*hy are we the way we are? Why are we so self-centered and self-absorbed? Is this how God made us—petty, proud, and perverse?

The answer to the final question, of course, is no. God made us to be just like Him. Sometimes we hear people say, "Well, isn't she the spitting image of her mother." I'm not sure what spitting has to do with it, but most of us have heard the saying before. It means "She looks and act just like her mother. Anyone can tell that one came from and belongs to the other." In the same way, we were created to be the spitting image of God.

This doesn't mean God has a body and is about six foot three with blue eyes. It means that Adam and Eve were created to have the character of God and live on earth as God's representatives. We are more than a mass of molecules. We are more than the sum of blood, bones, tissues, organs, and skin. Of all His creatures, we are unique in that we can know God, hear from God, communicate with God, and have union with God. This is not true of a giraffe or a beetle or a mourning dove. We are more important, more intelligent, and more magnificent than plants, animals, mountains, and microbes, because we are unique among God's creation, made just a little lower than the angels, crowned with glory and honor (Ps. 8:5). We have souls. We were made to know God and look like God. That's how things were in the beginning.

But all of this has changed. Let's go back to the garden of Eden. The Tree of the Knowledge of Good and Evil was a probationary tree. It was there to test Adam. "Do this and live," God said. "Disobey and die." Adam disobeyed, so he died . . . and so Paradise died and so we die.

As a result of the fall, shame enters the world—Adam and Eve realize they are naked (3:7). Fear enters the world—Adam and Eve hide from God (3:10). Blame enters the world—the man blames God for giving him the woman, and the woman blames the serpent for deceiving her (3:11–13). Pain enters the world (3:16). Relationships break down (3:16). Just making it in life will be a chore (3:17).

Because of Adam's sin, God curses the serpent, curses the woman, curses the man, and curses the ground. So serpents slither, women have pain in childbirth, men are frustrated by work, and the earth produces thorns and thistles. All of creation, in other words, is subjected to futility, so that creation itself now eagerly awaits freedom from its decay (Rom. 8:20–25).

Moreover, because of Adam's sin, human nature has been tarnished. J. C. Ryle, the Anglican bishop from the nineteenth century, said we are like smashed-up temples. There is still a trace of original splendor as creatures made in the image of God, but the temple that was once glorious now has windows broken and columns crumbling and doorways smashed in. We are not what we once were.

The Catechism makes clear that we are not just imitators of our first parents, sinning like Adam and Eve. We are born with a warped nature, tainted with an inherent and inherited corruption from conception on. We absolutely must get this right if we are to make sense of the Catechism and Christianity. Our fundamental problem is not bad parents, bad schools, bad friends, or bad circumstances. Our fundamental problem is a bad heart. And every single one of us is born into the world with it.

"All right, all right," you may be saying, "I am a bad person. I make mistakes. I'm not perfect. I agree. But I'm not *that* bad." Not so fast, says the Catechism. We are not just flawed. We are, to use the theological terminology, totally depraved. This doesn't mean we are bad all the time or as bad as we possibly could be. And this doesn't mean unregenerate people are incapable of morally outstanding acts. Total depravity means two things: (1) We are bad through and through (in head and heart and will), and (2) we are unable to do anything truly righteous because our "good" acts do not come from faith and do not aim at the glory of God.

Here's the bottom line: We are inclined toward evil (Gen. 6:5). All of us like sheep have gone astray (Isa. 53:6). Even our righteous deeds are as filthy rags before the Lord (Isa. 64:6 KJV).

That's a lot of bad news, even for a section that is supposed to be all about misery. But, according to Answer 8, there is hope. We are unable to do good and are bent toward evil, *unless* we are born again by the Spirit of God. Unfortunately, the phrase "born again" has become just another sociopolitical category. We have forgotten where it comes from. Jesus, borrowing from the prophet Ezekiel, is the one who first used the phrase. "You must be born again," He told Nicodemus (John 3:7).

We must not forget this command from Jesus. Yes, Jesus wants us to love, to forgive, to pray, to be humble, to do justice, and to love mercy. But we must not forget the fountainhead command from which the river of obedience flows. Trying to live a Jesus life won't help us get into heaven and it will only discourage us over the long haul if we are not born again. This is where well-meaning socially minded Christians sometimes get off track. They want the world to live like Jesus, but they forget that we can't live like Jesus unless the Spirit of Jesus first changes us.

We must be given a new heart. We must be regenerated. We must be converted. We must be changed. The Christian life—the life of faith in God, hope in Christ, and love for others—necessitates, first of all, a life that has been given a supernatural new start by the Holy Spirit. We must be born again.

ℒord's Day 4

9. Q. BUT DOESN'T GOD DO US AN INJUSTICE BY REQUIRING IN HIS LAW WHAT WE ARE UNABLE TO DO?

A. No, God created humans with the ability to keep the law. They, however, tempted by the devil, in reckless disobedience, robbed themselves and all their descendants of these gifts.

10. Q. WILL GOD PERMIT SUCH DISOBEDIENCE AND REBELLION TO GO UNPUNISHED?

A. Certainly not. He is terribly angry about the sin we are born with as well as the sins we personally commit. As a just judge He punishes them now and in eternity. He has declared: "Cursed is everyone who does not continue to do everything written in the Book of the Law."

11. Q. BUT ISN'T GOD ALSO MERCIFUL?

A. God is certainly merciful, but He is also just. His justice demands that sin, committed against His supreme majesty, be punished with the supreme penalty—eternal punishment of body and soul.

We Love Justice,
and So Does God

*I*f we are unable to obey God's law, why is God upset with us when we break it? That's the gist of Question 9, and it's not a dumb question. If you told your eight-year-old girl to fly to the moon and she didn't get more than four inches off the ground, you wouldn't spank her, would you? If you did, you'd be a pretty rotten parent. In fact, your friends would ask, "Why in the world are you commanding your daughter to fly to the moon anyway?" It's not fair to demand of others what they are totally and inherently unable to accomplish. So how can God be fair and still punish humans for violating a standard they have no ability to keep?

One answer to this question is to consider what God can do for those who trust in Him. According to Scripture, we are not just sinking in sin, we are dead in trespasses. But, thankfully, God doesn't leave us there. He converts our hearts, grants us faith, and gives us new life in Christ. In other words, a humble heart will submit to God in whatever He commands, but an equally believing heart will trust that God can give us the ability by His Spirit to obey the commands that would otherwise be impossible for us. Our inability is real, but God can overcome our corruption and make us willing and able to live for Him.

That is not, however, the answer the Catechism gives in Answers 9 and 10. Heidelberg's response is to point us to the federal headship of Adam. Adam was our representative, the head of the human race, such that if he would have obeyed God's probationary command and kept the covenant of works, he and his descendants would have lived. In a mysterious way, we were all *in Adam* when he sinned, just as believers are *in Christ*, participating in His death and resurrection. Therefore, *in Adam* we all had our chance at an obedience that was within our grasp. But since Adam disobeyed, and the rest of humanity with him, Adam and his offspring face spiritual and physical death.

This means we are born with original sin *and* original guilt. Original sin refers to the sinful nature we inherited from Adam. Original guilt refers to the culpability we are born with as those who participated with Adam in his sin. So we are by nature not just morally tainted but children of wrath, deserving of God's punishment, even before we actually sin in our flesh (Eph. 2:3). Romans 5:12 says, "Therefore, just as sin came into the world through one man, and death through sin, and so death spread to all men because all sinned—" When Paul says "all sinned," he doesn't mean "all have sinned in our lifetimes." He means, "all sinned in Adam in the garden of Eden." Sin came into the world through Adam. Death came as a result of that sin. And death spread to everyone else in the human race because everyone else in the human race sinned in Adam at that moment in Eden in Genesis 3.

We know this is what Paul means because in verse 18 he compares the one trespass (Adam eating the fruit) with the one act of righteousness (Christ's death on the cross). Just as the one act of disobedience brought condemnation and death through our union with Adam (and not just as a result of our subsequent sin), so also the one act of obedience brings justification and life through our union with Christ, and not as a result of subsequent good works.

It's like playing fantasy football. In fantasy football you pick your players, and when they get a lot of yards or score a touchdown, your fantasy team gets points. You're not physically doing anything. You're sitting on your duff watching the game. You didn't run into the end zone. But yet you talk about *your* team, *your* points, *your* wins and losses. The players are your representatives. That's Paul's argument in Romans. Every human being past, present, and future had Adam on his fantasy team, which means we all lost. When Adam sinned, we sinned. So Adam's punishment of death is our punishment too.

To summarize, then, God has the right to judge us, now and in eternity, for two reasons: (1) we have broken the law that originally we had the ability to keep, and (2) we sinned in Adam and deserve death for that sin just as Adam did.

With all this talk of guilt and judgment, Question 11 anticipates a reasonable objection: "But isn't God also merciful?" This question has a familiar ring to it. I can't count the number of times I've talked to Christians, not to mention non-Christians, who balk at the thought of God's wrath. "Sinners in the hands of an angry God?" they scoff. "We're past that fire-and-brimstone, puritanical stuff. The God I believe in is a God of love."

But divine love without divine wrath is meaningless. When we minimize God's justice, we do not exalt His mercy, we undermine it. God's mercy exhibits its full power and sweetness when we see it not merely as a general goodwill to all people, but as the means by which God's people are rescued, in Christ, from their just wrath and condemnation.

God's justice demands that sin and rebellion and idolatry not go unpunished. We often struggle to embrace God's right to execute justice, but when the referee blows a call against our team, we'll stand up and yell at the television. When our insurance company refuses to pay what the policy says they should, we'll get downright indignant. We all have a sense of justice. But somehow we don't think God can be concerned for justice when He is wronged.

We need a God who makes moral judgments. If He loves everyone in exactly the same way, what does His love really mean, and what does it mean to be loved by God? Our universe would make no sense and the pain of injustice would be even greater if we did not have a God who recognizes right from wrong and judges the wicked. Be glad, though: Just as we love justice, so does God.

$\mathscr{L}$ord's Day 5

12. Q. ACCORDING TO GOD'S RIGHTEOUS JUDGMENT WE DESERVE PUNISHMENT BOTH IN THIS WORLD AND FOREVER AFTER: HOW THEN CAN WE ESCAPE PUNISHMENT AND RETURN TO GOD'S FAVOR?

A. God requires that His justice be satisfied. Therefore the claims of His justice must be paid in full, either by ourselves or another.

13. Q. CAN WE PAY THIS DEBT OURSELVES?

A. Certainly not. Actually, we increase our guilt every day.

14. Q. CAN ANOTHER CREATURE—ANY AT ALL—PAY THIS DEBT FOR US?

A. No. To begin with, God will not punish another creature for what a human is guilty of. Besides, no mere creature can bear the weight of God's eternal anger against sin and release others from it.

15. Q. WHAT KIND OF MEDIATOR AND DELIVERER SHOULD WE LOOK FOR THEN?

A. One who is truly human and truly righteous, yet more powerful than all creatures, that is, one who is also true God.

Yet Not Two, but One

Although the word is not mentioned, *hell* is the subject of Lord's Day 5. Many Christians today would prefer not to think about hell. They ignore it, deny it, or practice a studied agnosticism about the subject. Many of us are squeamish about God's wrath and reticent to share a gospel message that has to do with salvation from coming judgment. Certainly, we need balance. The implications of the gospel ought to lead to love of God and good for the world. But too often, the gospel is explained first of all as a message about selfless love, service, and dying for others. True, that is the heart of the gospel, but we are to proclaim the selfless love, service, and *dying for others by the Christ* who came to rescue *sinners*.

Before we talk about rescuing the planet (reclaiming America for Christ on the right, and joining the ONE campaign on the left), we need to hear how Jesus came to deliver sinners. From what I've seen and read, the interest in missions among young people is trending away from saving souls and toward saving the world. The interest is too often social to the exclusion of spiritual. The two don't have to be at odds with each other. Those who deal with the "spiritual" must not ignore the "social," and those who engage the "social" must fully embrace the "spiritual."

What we don't want are Christians who admirably try to relieve suffering in the world, but are indifferent toward eternal suffering. Every Christian engaged in mission—be it medical, educational, agricultural, or just plain being a good neighbor—should care about real-life pain and long for opportunities to share the good news that every person needs to hear. Unless, of course, Jesus was wrong and there is no reason to fear Him who can throw body and soul into hell (Matt. 10:28).

The Catechism reorients us to the crisis of the human condition: On our own, God is not for us but against us. God's wrath cannot be wished away from the pages of Scripture. Even in passages like Matthew 25 where Jesus commands us to feed and clothe the least of our brothers, He also warns against being shut out of the coming wedding feast (v. 10), being cast into the outer darkness (v. 30), and going away into eternal punishment (v. 46). With sober gravity we must confess that hell is real and people will go there.

God's justice means that we deserve punishment now and later. It is impossible for God to lie. It is impossible for Him to change. And it is impossible for Him to violate His own justice. He cannot let lawbreakers go free with the wave of His hand in some act of tolerance or inclusivity. Sin must be atoned for and sinners must be punished.

There are two options, then, if God is to be true to Himself and maintain justice in the universe. We can pay this debt or someone else can pay it for us. Question and Answer 13 quickly disposes of the first option. We can't do enough to atone for our sins, both because we are finite and cannot pay for our offense against an infinite God and because each day we sin more and see our guilt increase. "You load sixteen tons and what do you get?" asks the old folk song. "Another day older and deeper in debt." The same is true in our spiritual lives. We can't pay the debt we owe to God. The more we try to dig ourselves out, the deeper our pit gets.

"What about another creature?" asks Question 14. Can something else in the created universe—anything at all—pay our debt for us? The answer again is no. First of all, God is fair and will not punish another creature for human sin. Only flesh and blood can save flesh and blood (Heb. 2:14–18). To put it another way, it takes a member of the family to save the family. Second, another creature paying our debt would have the same problem as any human—insufficient funds. The weight of God's eternal anger is more than any animal, saint, or angel can bear.

As you can see, Heidelberg's logic is marching us in a straight line to Christ. Our Deliverer is not named until Lord's Day 5, but that's the only option Question 15 leaves on the table. If God will not punish a non-human for human sin, and yet, a human cannot bear the weight of divine wrath, the only one who can deliver us is a being who is both human and divine. We need a mediator who can lay a hand on us both (Job 9:33). We need a righteous Man to save fallen men and a divine Man to bear the curse of God. We need "One who is truly human and truly righteous . . . who is also true God."

It took the church a few centuries of heresies to safeguard this biblical truth from error. Almost all the early heresies dealt somehow with the person of Christ, either denying His full deity (Arianism), or His full manhood (Docetism), or confusing the two (Eutychianism), or splitting the two (Nestorianism). As attractive as the compromise solutions seemed at the time, nothing other than full-throated orthodoxy would do, because nothing other than a God-man can save men from God. We need a bridge that goes far enough in both directions, spanning the gulf that exists between a holy God and rebellious people. We need a Mediator, as the Athanasian Creed says, who is "God and human" yet "not two, but one."

Lord's Day 6

16. Q. WHY MUST HE BE TRULY HUMAN AND TRULY RIGHTEOUS?

A. God's justice demands that human nature, which has sinned, must pay for its sin; but a sinner could never pay for others.

17. Q. WHY MUST HE ALSO BE TRUE GOD?

A. So that, by the power of His divinity, He might bear the weight of God's anger in His humanity and earn for us and restore to us righteousness and life.

18. Q. AND WHO IS THIS MEDIATOR—TRUE GOD AND AT THE SAME TIME TRULY HUMAN AND TRULY RIGHTEOUS?

A. Our Lord Jesus Christ, who was given us to set us completely free and to make us right with God.

19. Q. HOW DO YOU COME TO KNOW THIS?

A. The holy gospel tells me. God Himself began to reveal the gospel already in Paradise; later, He proclaimed it by the holy patriarchs and prophets, and portrayed it by the sacrifices and other ceremonies of the law; finally, He fulfilled it through His own dear Son.

The Substitute
Who Satisfies

Several theological words are used to describe Christ's work on the cross, all of them important, and all alluded to in Q/A 16–18. *Expiation* means that Christ's death removed our sin and guilt (Q/A 16). *Redemption* means Christ's death ransomed us from the curse of the law and the punishment and power of sin (Q/A 18). *Reconciliation* means Christ's death restored our relationship with God (Q/A 18). *Propitiation* means Christ's death appeased or placated the wrath of God (Q/A 17).

All four of these terms (and there are others) capture an essential and biblical aspect of the cross. The best news about Jesus is that through Him we are forgiven of our sins, set free from the law, made right with God, and can stand confident before our Creator.

All this is announced to us in the *gospel* (Q/A 19). The gospel is not a summons to kingdom living or a message about what we can do for God or a description of our efforts at cultural transformation. The gospel, according to Paul's summary in 1 Corinthians 15, is the good news that Jesus Christ died for our sins and rose again on the third day. I mention all this vocabulary because Lord's Day 6 leads us to it, and because the ideas safeguarded by these words are often denied, minimized, or marginalized as one "theory" of the atonement. Which leads me to a story.

A couple of years ago I found myself writing a long letter to a church leader in my denomination. I was writing to respond to a critique this individual had offered (anonymously) against a group I am affiliated with. The overall critique was intelligent and asked some good questions. But the most surprising and disappointing sentence I read was this one: *"I actually find no place in Scripture itself that speaks of the wrath of God being directed on Jesus at the cross."*

My response, which relates directly to the atonement, the gospel, and Lord's Day 6, went like this:

"This is a shocking statement [the one in italics above]. I've read it over a dozen times to make sure I understand it correctly. If the sentence is correct, then most of our churches are proclaiming something other than the gospel. Is not the message preached in hundreds of our churches simply this: God created us in His image; because of the fall we are by nature children of wrath; left to our own we cannot stand before a holy God; we deserve to be punished for offending this God; but in love God sent His Son to bear our sins and face the penalty we deserved; God's wrath was poured out on Jesus and Jesus' righteousness is imputed to us by faith—is this not the gospel? Of course, there's more to be said about the Christian story, but certainly not less than this. I can't help but be saddened that someone in the Reformed Church in America would deny such a central tenet of the gospel, one that is reiterated numerous times in our confessions.

"I can find numerous places in Scripture where we are taught, explicitly or implicitly, that the wrath of God was directed on Jesus at the cross. One thinks of the Passover in Exodus 12. Penal substitution lies at the heart of the Passover—God poured out His wrath on the slain lamb instead of His people. Surely, this line of thinking is present in John's gospel where John the Baptist confesses about Jesus: "The Lamb of God, who takes away the sin of the world!" (John 1:29). I also see the wrath of God poured out on Jesus prefigured in the Day of Atonement ritual of Leviticus 16. In addition, Isaiah 53 poignantly touches on the same theme. Jesus, as the Suffering Servant, was pierced for our transgressions and crushed for our iniquities. It was the Lord's will to crush Him, pouring out His wrath on His Servant.

"Similarly, Mark 10:45 teaches that Jesus gave His life as a ransom for many. This ransom was paid, not to Satan as some medieval theologians wrongly taught, but to God the Father as a fragrant offering and sacrifice to Him (Eph. 5:2). In Mark 10:38 Jesus asked His disciples "Are you able to drink the cup I drink?" And in Gethsemane, Jesus pleaded with His Father, "remove this cup from me" (Mark 14:36). Surely Jesus was thinking of passages like Ps. 75:8; Isaiah 51:17; Jeremiah 25:15–16, Ezekiel 23:32–34; and Habakkuk 2:16; all of which speak of drinking the cup of God's wrath. John 3:14–18 teaches that God sent His Son to be lifted up on the cross (like the snake lifted up in the wilderness, which saved people from God's judgment) so that the wrath of God would not remain on those who believe. Romans 3:21–26 teaches that Christ was set forth as a sacrifice of atonement (literally "propitiation"; see Leon Morris's classic work *The Apostolic Preaching of the Cross*,[7] which establishes that *hilasterion* refers to propitiation, contra C. H. Dodd) turning aside God's wrath by suffering in our place as our substitute. Romans 5:8–9 argues that Christ died for us while we were God's enemies, so that we might be saved by Him from the wrath of God. Galatians 3:13 says Christ became a curse for us, bearing the penalty we deserved as lawbreakers. First John 4:10 teaches that God sent His Son to be a propitiation for our sins (see also 1 John 2:2; Heb. 2:17). And on and on."

There is nothing more important in Christian theology than our theology of the cross. We must speak clearly that the heart of the gospel is the good news of divine self-satisfaction through divine self-substitution. Never compromise on the cross. Never dilute the message of the cross. And never stop glorying in the cross where Christ accepted the penalties that should belong to us so that we can claim the blessings that would otherwise belong only to Him.[8]

Lord's Day 7

20. Q. ARE ALL SAVED THROUGH CHRIST JUST AS ALL WERE LOST THROUGH ADAM?

A. No. Only those are saved who by true faith are grafted into Christ and accept all His blessings.

21. Q. WHAT IS TRUE FAITH?

A. True faith is not only a knowledge and conviction that everything God reveals in His Word is true; it is also a deep-rooted assurance, created in me by the Holy Spirit through the gospel, that, out of sheer grace earned for us by Christ, not only others, but I too, have had my sins forgiven, have been made forever right with God, and have been granted salvation.

22. Q. WHAT THEN MUST A CHRISTIAN BELIEVE?

A. Everything God promises us in the gospel. That gospel is summarized for us in the articles of our Christian faith—a creed beyond doubt, and confessed throughout the world.

23. Q. WHAT ARE THESE ARTICLES?

A. I believe in God, the Father almighty, creator of heaven and earth. I believe in Jesus Christ, His only Son, our Lord, who was conceived by the Holy Spirit and born of the virgin Mary. He suffered under Pontius Pilate, was crucified, died, and was buried; He descended to hell. The third day He rose again from the dead. He ascended to heaven and is seated at the right hand of God the Father almighty. From there He will come to judge the living and the dead. I believe in the Holy Spirit, the holy catholic church, the communion of saints, the forgiveness of sins, the resurrection of the body, and the life everlasting. Amen.

True Faith

The whole story of Christianity can be summarized in two Adams. The first Adam—the one defying God in the garden of Eden—as a representative head for the entire human race disobeyed and plunged every other mortal into sin and misery. The second Adam—the one crying to God in the garden of Gethsemane—as a representative head for all the elect obeyed even unto death and purchased redemption for all who believe.

Redemption is not a right but a blessing. Not all will be saved. Although the fall of humanity was universal, salvation is not. It is only by faith that we are joined to Christ and share in all that His salvation accomplished. Without faith, we are dead in trespasses and sin. As Jesus explained to Nicodemus, "Whoever believes in him [the Son of God] is not condemned, but whoever does not believe is condemned already, because he has not believed in the name of the only Son of God" (John 3:18).

But what is true faith? Anyone within earshot of the church has heard plenty about faith. We are saved by faith. We stand by faith. We must examine ourselves to see if we are in the faith. We go to heaven with faith; we go somewhere else without faith. But what is true faith? The Catechism gives one of the best answers you'll find anywhere.

Faith is "knowledge and conviction" (Answer 21). Here we have the proverbial head and heart of the Christian faith. True faith is knowledge: We must understand something and know something about God and the gospel; we are not saved by a content-less Christ. And true faith is conviction: We must trust and embrace and feel something of the glory of the knowledge we possess. Even the demons have good theology (James 2:19). Knowledge is necessary, but it is not enough.

Faith is also "a deep-rooted assurance." It is not arrogant, but it is con-fident. We should have mercy on those who doubt (Jude 22), but doubt is not the goal. We want a faith that is not constantly wandering and won-dering but sure and established. Faith is the assurance of things hoped for, the conviction of things not seen (Heb. 11:1).

Faith is "created . . . by the Holy Spirit through the gospel." Genuine trust in God does not come by virtue of superior intellect or by luck of a credulous personality. It is the work of God's Spirit birthed in us through the hearing of the good news about Christ. The salvation we receive by faith is a gift, and so is faith itself.

Faith is humble. It puts an end to all boasting except in the cross, and puts to flight any thoughts of merit except that which was won for us by Christ.

Faith is personal. Faith is not trust in an abstract principle that God is love or that Jesus died on the cross for sinners. Faith is personal, believing that God loves me, that Jesus died for me. Faith trusts that God did not send His Son merely to do something wonderful for people out there in the world. He sent His Son to live and die in my place. Salvation is more than a concept, it's a conviction. True faith believes "*I* am forgiven, *I* am right with God, and *I* will live forever."

But if this is what faith is like, what does faith believe? We are not saved by believing anything in particular, as if God just wanted people to be generally optimistic and full of wishful thinking. The object of our faith is the whole point. Our faith, no matter how sincere, will be sin-cerely mistaken if it trusts in something other than gospel. The gospel, after all, is the power of salvation to everyone who believes (Rom. 1:16).

But *the gospel* is not an easy term to define. Most foundationally, it refers to the good news about Jesus' death and resurrection (1 Cor. 15:1–8), but more broadly it can be shorthand for the whole message and story of the Christian faith (2 Tim. 1:8; 2:8). It's in the second sense that the Cate-chism understands the "gospel" in Answer 22. The gospel is what one must believe in order to be a Christian.

We've all heard the saying, "In essentials unity. In nonessentials liberty. And in all things charity." Every Christian likes this saying, but no one quite agrees on which things are which. The Heidelberg Catechism, standing in a long line of church tradition and understanding, teaches that a good summary of the essentials can be found in the Apostles' Creed, shown in Answer 23. It would be unwise to say there is nothing else essential outside of these articles. Other controversies were yet to come, and other key doctrines would need to be defined. The creeds of Nicea and Chalcedon, for example, were just as important in defining the Christian faith in the early church. Likewise, it would be unwise to say there is nothing else outside of the Apostles' Creed that is worth talking about or declaring, because even the Heidelberg Catechism does not hesitate to explain other doctrines and "take sides" on other theological matters.

But if you are looking for a succinct summary of the essentials of the faith, there is no better starting point than the Apostles' Creed. The Christian faith, if it is to be Christian in any meaningful, historic sense of the term, cannot contain less than the Apostles' Creed. In a world where theology is often ignored and boundary setting is abhorred, we must not forget that there are things a Christian must believe.

*L*ord's Day 8

24. Q. HOW ARE THESE ARTICLES DIVIDED?

A. Into three parts: God the Father and our creation; God the Son and our deliverance; God the Holy Spirit and our sanctification.

25. Q. SINCE THERE IS BUT ONE GOD, WHY DO YOU SPEAK OF THREE: FATHER, SON, AND HOLY SPIRIT?

A. Because that is how God has revealed Himself in His Word: these three distinct persons are one, true, eternal God.

The Most Important Doctrine You Never Think About

*I*f any doctrine makes Christianity Christian, then surely it is the doctrine of the Trinity. The three great ecumenical creeds—the Apostles' Creed, the Nicene Creed, and the Athanasian Creed—are all structured around our three-in-one God, underlying the essential importance of Trinitarian theology.

Augustine once commented about the Trinity that "in no other subject is error more dangerous, or inquiry more laborious, or the discovery of truth more profitable."[9] More recently, Sinclair Ferguson has reflected on "the rather obvious thought that when his disciples were about to have the world collapse in on them, our Lord spent so much time in the Upper Room speaking to them about the mystery of the Trinity. If anything could underline the necessity of Trinitarianism for practical Christianity, that must surely be it!"[10]

Yet when it comes to the doctrine of the Trinity, most Christians are poor in their understanding, poorer in their articulation, and poorest of all in seeing any way in which the doctrine matters in real life. One theologian said, tongue in cheek, "The Trinity is a matter of five notions or properties, four relations, three persons, two processions, one substance or nature, and no understanding."[11] All the talk of essence and persons and co-this and co-that seems like theological gobbledy-gook reserved for philosophers and scholars—maybe for thinky bookish types, but certainly not for moms and mechanics and middle-class college students.

So, let's see, I have about eight hundred words left in this chapter to explain what the doctrine of the Trinity means, where it is found in the Bible, and why it matters.

First, *what does the doctrine mean*? The doctrine of the Trinity can be summarized in seven statements. (1) There is only one God. (2) The Father is God. (3) The Son is God. (4) The Holy Spirit is God. (5) The Father is not the Son. (6) The Son is not the Holy Spirit. (7) The Holy Spirit is not the Father. All of the creedal formulations and theological jargon and philosophical apologetics have to do with safeguarding each one of these statements and doing so without denying any of the other six. The Athanasian Creed puts it this way: "Now this is the catholic [i.e., universal] faith: That we worship one God in trinity and the trinity in unity, neither blending their persons, nor dividing their essence. For the person of the Father is a distinct person, the person of the Son is another, and that of the Holy Spirit, still another. But the divinity of the Father, Son, and Holy Spirit is one, their glory equal, their majesty coeternal."

The two key words here are "essence" and "persons." When you read "essence," think "Godness." All three persons of the Trinity share the same "Godness." One is not more God than another. None is more essentially divine than the rest. When you read "persons," think "a particular individual distinct from the others." Theologians use these terms because they are trying to find a way to express the relationship of three beings who are equally and uniquely God, but not three Gods. That's why we get this obscure language of essence and persons. We want to be true to the biblical witness that there is an indivisibility and unity of God, even though Father, Son, and Holy Spirit can all be rightly called God. The persons are not three Gods; rather, they dwell in communion with each other as they subsist in the divine nature without being compounded or confused.

Confusing, isn't it? Sometimes it's easier to understand what we believe by stating what we don't believe. Orthodox Trinitarianism rejects *monarchianism*, which believes in only one person (mono) and maintains that the Son and the Spirit subsist in the divine essence as impersonal attributes, not as distinct and divine persons. Orthodox Trinitarianism rejects *modalism*, which believes that Father, Son, and Holy Spirit are different names for the same God acting in different roles (like the well-intentioned but misleading "water, vapor, ice" analogy). Orthodox Trinitarianism rejects *Arianism*, which denies the full deity of Christ. And finally, orthodox Trinitarianism rejects all forms of *tritheism*, which teach that the three members of the Godhead are, to quote a leading Mormon apologist, "three distinct Beings, three separate Gods."[12]

Second, *where is the doctrine of the Trinity found in the Bible?* Although the word *Trinity* is famously absent from Scripture, the theology behind the word can be found in a surprising number of verses. For starters there are verses that speak of God's oneness (Deut. 6:4; Isa. 44:6; 1 Tim. 1:17). Then there are the myriad of passages which demonstrate that God is Father (e.g., John 6:27; Titus 1:4). Next, we have the scores of texts that prove the deity of Jesus Christ, the Son—passages like John 1: ("the word was God"), John 8:58 ("before Abraham was born, I am"), Colossians 2:9 (NIV) ("in Christ all the fullness of the Deity lives in bodily form"), Hebrews 1:3 (NIV) ("The Son is the radiance of God's glory and the exact imprint of his being"), Titus 2:13 ("our great God and Savior Jesus Christ")—not to mention the explicit worship Christ willingly received from His disciples (Luke 24:52; John 20:28) and the charges of blasphemy leveled against Him for making Himself equal with God (Mark 2:7). Then we have similar texts that assume the deity of the Holy Spirit, calling Him an "eternal Spirit" (Heb. 9:14) and using "God" interchangeably with the "Holy Spirit" (1 Cor. 3:16; 6:19; Acts 5:3–4) without a second thought.

The shape of Trinitarian orthodoxy is finally rounded off by texts that hint at the plurality of persons in the Godhead (Gen. 1:1–3, 26; Psalm 2:7; Dan. 7), texts like 1 Corinthians 8:6, which places Jesus Christ as Lord right in the middle of Jewish Shema, and dozens of texts that speak of the Father, Son, and Holy Spirit in the same breath, equating the three in rank, while assuming distinction of personhood (Matt. 28:19; Gal. 4:6; 1 Cor. 12:4–6; 1 Peter 1:1–2; 2 Cor. 1:21–22; 13:14; Eph. 1:13–14; 2:18, 20–22; 3:14–17; 4:4–6; 5:18–20; 6:10–18).

The doctrine of the Trinity, as summarized in the seven statements earlier, is not a philosophical concoction by some overzealous and overintelligent early theologians, but one of the central planks of orthodoxy that can be shown, explicitly or implicitly, from a multitude of biblical texts.

Third, *why does any of this matter?* There are lots of reasons, but in

Trinitarian fashion let me mention just three.[13] One, the Trinity matters for creation. God, unlike the gods in other ancient creation stories, did not need to go outside Himself to create the universe. Instead, the Word and the Spirit were like His own two hands (to use Irenaeus's famous phrase) in fashioning the cosmos. God created by speaking (the Word) as the Spirit hovered over the chaos. Creation, like regeneration, is a Trinitarian act, with God working by the agency of the Word spoken and the mysterious movement of the Holy Spirit.

Two, the Trinity matters for evangelism and cultural engagement. I've heard it said that the two main rivals to a Christian worldview at present are Islam and postmodernism. Islam emphasizes unity—unity of language, culture, and expression—without allowing much variance for diversity. Postmodernism, on the other hand, emphasizes diversity—diversity of opinion, beliefs, and background—without attempting to see things in any kind of meta-unity. Christianity, with its understanding of God as three in one, allows for diversity and unity. If God exists in three distinct persons who all share the same essence, then it is possible to hope that God's creation may exhibit stunning variety and individuality while still holding together in a genuine oneness.

Three, the Trinity matters for relationships. We worship a God who is in constant and eternal relationship with Himself as Father, Son, and Holy Spirit. *Community* is a buzz word in American culture, but it is only in a Christian framework that communion and interpersonal community are seen as expressions of the eternal nature of God. Likewise, it is only with a Trinitarian God that love can be an eternal attribute of God. Without a plurality of persons in the Godhead, we would be forced to think that God created humans so that He might show love and know love, thereby making love a created thing (and God a needy deity). But with a biblical understanding of the Trinity, we can say that God did not create in order to be loved, but rather, created out of the overflow of the perfect love that had always existed among Father, Son, and Holy Spirit who ever live in perfect and mutual relationship and delight.

26. Q. WHAT DO YOU BELIEVE WHEN YOU SAY, "I BELIEVE IN GOD, THE FATHER ALMIGHTY, CREATOR OF HEAVEN AND EARTH"?

A. That the eternal Father of our Lord Jesus Christ, who out of nothing created heaven and earth and everything in them, who still upholds and rules them by His eternal counsel and providence, is my God and Father because of Christ His Son. I trust Him so much that I do not doubt He will provide whatever I need for body and soul, and He will turn to my good whatever adversity He sends me in this sad world. He is able to do this because He is almighty God; He desires to do this because He is a faithful Father.

Your Father Is God

*B*esides being ancient, ecumenical (in the good sense), and biblical, the Apostles' Creed is catchy. I'm not sure if you can dance to it (haven't tried), but it does have a cadence that makes congregational recitation intuitively doable. The first line rolls off the tongue nicely: "I believe in God, the Father almighty, creator of heaven and earth." But behind the familiar language and rhythm, there are a number of important theological points to be made. I count at least seven.

First, our heavenly Father is the *eternal* Father of our Lord Jesus Christ. There never was when Christ was not (contra Arianism), and there never was when the Father was not a father to the Son and the Son a son to the Father. God has always been the God and Father of the Son, even before the incarnation. The single characteristic of fatherhood defines and describes Him in a way that is essential, irreducible, and eternal.

Second, God created the world *ex nihilo*, which is Latin for "out of nothing." In the beginning there was God and nothing else. "By faith we understand that the universe was created by the word of God, so that what is seen was not made out of things that are visible" (Heb. 11:3). No stars, no sky, no light, no sun, no creatures, no water, no dust—nothing. It's almost impossible to comprehend. We can fathom an uninhabited world, even a universe filled with an endless expanse of darkness, but prior to Genesis 1:1 there wasn't even a dark sky. There was nothing but nothingness. The only something was an invisible, spiritual, eternal God. And after countless eons of inter-Trinitarian bliss, God decided He would make something. He simply commanded and it came forth, even though there was no "it" to come forth prior to God's voice making it so (Ps. 33:6).

Third, the same God who created the universe out of nothing still upholds and rules His creation by His counsel and providence. If the Christian belief in creation *ex nihilo* rules out dualism (God and matter have always existed side by side) and pantheism (God is the universe and the universe is God), then our belief in providence rules out deism. God did not create the world like some cosmic watchmaker, winding it up and then leaving it to tick-tock by itself. Instead, God still rules over heaven and earth, superintending and guiding them by His fatherly hand.

Fourth, this creator of the universe is my God and Father. Most kids go through a phase where they brag about their dads. "My dad can throw a football about a mile!" "So, my dad makes like a million trillion dollars!" "Well, my dad reads a lot of books!" We've all heard these boasts (except for the last one, but my boys need something to say too). Consider the boast you could make if your father threw all the miles a football could ever travel, and owned all the money in every bank account in the world, and knew every fact in every book that's been written or ever will be written. That would be one great dad. And that's your Father in heaven. We have often heard that God is our Father, which is true, but we don't always remember that the opposite is just as true: your Father is God.

Fifth, God is my Father because of Christ, His Son. The old liberal credo made much of "the universal fatherhood of God." But as nice as it sounds, God is not the Father of all. He is God over all (even though many do not worship Him), and Lord over all (though many do not submit to Him), and in one sense He may be called the Father of all in that all people owe their existence to God. But in the deeper sense of the title—the way Jesus used it—God is not the Father of all. He is only Father to those who have Christ for their brother (Heb. 2:10–17). We are children of God, not by right of human birth but by virtue of divine adoption. It is those who receive Jesus and believe in His name who are given the right to be called children of God, children born not of the flesh but of God (John 1:12).

This may sound harsh to those outside the Christian faith, but if the Bible really taught "the universal fatherhood of God," where would the good news be in that? Let's see, Jesus came and died so you could be right with God and know Him as your loving heavenly Father, which of course is how He relates to everyone already. There's no offense in that, and no love either. Scripture teaches that because of God's love for us, while we were yet *sinners*, Christ died for us (Rom. 5:8). And it is only by virtue of Christ's death and resurrection we can receive "the Spirit of adoption as sons, by whom we cry, 'Abba! Father!'" (Rom. 8:15).

Sixth, therefore, we do not doubt His provision. All of this theology is moving us to trust. Because God created everything out of nothing, and because He still sustains His creation by His providence, and because the God who did and does all this is our Father by virtue of our union with Christ—because of all this, we can count on our God.

Seventh, He will turn to good whatever adversity He sends me. The Bible is not naïve about suffering. Trusting in God's provision does not mean we expect to float to heaven on flowery beds of ease. This is a "sad world" we live in, one in which God not only allows trouble but at times sends adversity to us. Trust, therefore, does not mean hoping for the absence of pain but believing in the purpose of pain. After all, if my almighty God is really almighty and my heavenly Father is really fatherly, then I should trust that He can and will do what is good for me in this sad world. Parents, don't you wish your kids had more faith in you and trusted that you knew what was best and were always on their side? I imagine God wants the same kind of faith for all of us.

27. Q. WHAT DO YOU UNDERSTAND BY THE PROVIDENCE OF
GOD?

A. Providence is the almighty and ever present power of God by
which He upholds, as with His hand, heaven and earth and all
creatures, and so rules them that leaf and blade, rain and drought,
fruitful and lean years, food and drink, health and sickness, prosperity and poverty—all things, in fact, come to us not by chance
but from His fatherly hand.

28. Q. HOW DOES THE KNOWLEDGE OF GOD'S CREATION
AND PROVIDENCE HELP US?

A. We can be patient when things go against us, thankful when
things go well, and for the future we can have good confidence in
our faithful God and Father that nothing will separate us from
His love. All creatures are so completely in His hand that without
His will they can neither move nor be moved.

All Things Come
from His Hand

*I*n the entire Catechism, Lord's Day 10 is my favorite. I absolutely love its poetic description of providence. *Sovereignty* is the word we hear more often. That's a good word too. But if people run out of the room crying whenever you talk to them about sovereignty, try using the word *providence*. God's providence is His sovereignty for us. As Eric Liddel's dad remarked in *Chariots of Fire*, God may be a dictator, but "Aye, He is a benign, loving dictator."

For many Christians, coming to grips with God's all-encompassing providence requires a massive shift in how they look at the world. It requires changing our vantage point—from seeing the cosmos as a place where man rules and God responds, to beholding a universe where God creates and constantly controls with sovereign love and providential power.

The definition of providence in the Catechism is stunning. "All things"—yes *all* things—"come to us not by chance but from His fatherly hand." I will sometimes ask seminary students being examined for ordination, "How would the Heidelberg Catechism, particularly Lord's Day 10, help you minister to someone who lost a loved one in Afghanistan or just lost a job?" I am usually disappointed to hear students who should be affirming the confessions of their denomination shy away from Heidelberg's strong, biblical language about providence. Like most of us, the students are much more at ease using passive language about God's permissive will or comfortable generalities about God being "in control" than they are about stating precisely and confidently to those in the midst of suffering "this has come from God's fatherly hand." And yet, that's what the Catechism, and more importantly the Bible, teaches.

Let me be clear: God's providence is not an excuse to act foolishly or sinfully. Herod and Pontius Pilate, though they did what God had planned beforehand, were still wicked conspirators (Acts 4:25–28). The Bible affirms human responsibility. But the Bible also affirms, much more massively and frequently than some imagine, God's power and authority over all things. The nations are under God's control (Pss. 2:1–4; 33:10), as is nature (Mark 4:41; Pss. 135:7; 147:18; 148:8), and animals (2 Kings 17:25; Dan. 6:22; Matt. 10:29). God is sovereign over Satan and evil spirits (Matt. 4:10; 2 Cor. 12:7–8; Mark 1:27). God uses wicked people for His plans—not just in a "bringing good out of evil" sort of way but in an active, intentional, "this was God's plan from the get-go" sort of way (Job 12:16; John 19:11; Gen. 45:8; Luke 22:22; Acts 4:27–28). God hardens hearts (Ex. 14:17; Josh. 11:20; Rom. 9:18). God sends trouble and calamity (Judg. 9:23; 1 Sam. 1:5; 16:14; 2 Sam. 24:1; 1 Kings 22:20–23; Isa. 45:6–7; 53:10; Amos 3:6; Ruth 1:20; Eccl. 7:14). God even puts to death (1 Sam. 2:6, 25; 2 Sam. 12:15; 2 Chron. 10:4, 14; Deut. 32:39). God does what He pleases and His purposes cannot be thwarted (Isa. 46:9–10; Dan. 4:34–35). In short, God guides all our steps and works all things after the counsel of His will (Prov. 16:33; 20:24; 21:2; Jer. 10:23; Ps. 139:16; Rom. 8:28; Eph. 1:11).

These verses are not meant to pound you into submission. I list dozens of verses for two reasons: First, so you can check this teaching out for yourself and see that God's superintendence is the unavoidable conclusion written large on the pages of Scripture. And second, so you will move past merely tolerating God's sovereignty to joyously embracing it.

Remember, Lord's Day 10 is explaining what the Creed means when it says, "I believe in God, the Father almighty, creator of heaven and earth." If God is the creator of all things and truly almighty, then He must continue to be almighty over all that He has created. And if God is a Father, then surely He exercises His authority over His creation and creatures for the good of His beloved children. Providence is nothing more than a belief in God the Father almighty, creator of heaven and earth, brought to bear on our present blessings and troubles and buoying our hope into the future.

You can look at providence through the lens of human autonomy and our idolatrous notions of freedom and see a mean God moving tsunamis and kings like chess pieces in some kind of perverse divine playtime. Or you can look at providence through the lens of Scripture and see a loving God counting the hairs on our heads and directing the sparrows in the sky so that we might live life unafraid. "What else can we wish for ourselves," Calvin wrote, "if not even one hair can fall from our head without His will?"[14] There are no accidents in your life. Every economic downturn, every phone call in the middle of the night, every oncology report has been sent to us from the God who sees all things, plans all things, and loves us more than we know. Whether it means the end of suffering or the extension of suffering, God in His providence is for us and not against us.

Providence is for our comfort. (1) We can be patient when things go against us. Joseph's imprisonment seemed pointless, but it makes sense now. Slavery in Egypt makes sense now. Killing the Messiah makes sense now. So maybe God knows what He's doing with the pain in our lives.

(2) We can be thankful when things go well. How often do we pray for safe travel or healing or a spouse or a job and then never get around to thanking God on the other side of blessing? If we truly believe in providence, we will view success and prosperity not as products of good upbringing, good looks, or good intelligence but ultimately as the unmerited favor of a good God.

(3) We can have confidence for the future. The fact is all your worries may come true, but God will never be untrue to you. He will always lead you and listen to you. God moves in mysterious ways, so we may not always understand why life is what it is. But it helps us face the future unafraid to know that nothing moves, however mysterious, except by the hand of that great Unmoved Mover who is our Father in heaven.

29. Q. WHY IS THE SON OF GOD CALLED "JESUS," MEANING "SAVIOR"?

A. Because He saves us from our sins. Salvation cannot be found in anyone else; it is futile to look for any salvation elsewhere.

30. Q. DO THOSE WHO LOOK FOR THEIR SALVATION AND SECURITY IN SAINTS, IN THEMSELVES, OR ELSEWHERE REALLY BELIEVE IN THE ONLY SAVIOR JESUS?

A. No. Although they boast of being His, by their deeds they deny the only Savior and deliverer, Jesus. Either Jesus is not a perfect Savior, or those who in true faith accept their Savior have in Him all they need for their salvation.

What's in a Name?

The Apostles' Creed is divided into three parts: God the Father, God the Son, and God the Holy Spirit. Having spent Lord's Days 9 and 10 on God the Father, the Catechism now directs its attention to God the Son in Lord's Days 11–19. The Catechism will take three Lord's Days (11–13) just to unpack the first line of the second part of the Creed: "I believe in Jesus Christ, His only Son, our Lord." This may seem like no-brainer land, making three weeks of reflection on this one line as thrilling as working your way through Turbo Tax, but the Catechism understands that in confessing Jesus as Christ, Son, and Lord, we are making the most important confession we can ever make. That's why the Catechism takes one Lord's Day each to explain what we mean by "Jesus," one day for "Christ," and one day for "Son" and "Lord" together.

Jesus was a very common name among Jewish males in the first century. From the evidence we have (over 2,500 named Jewish males in documents and inscriptions), scholars estimate that Jesus was the fourth most common name among Jewish men (about one out of twenty), behind Simeon/Simon, Joseph, and Judah. If you were a little boy in first-century Palestine, there would be a very good chance you'd meet a "Jesus" in your town or synagogue.

Jesus is the Greek equivalent of the Hebrew name *Joshua*, or *Jeshua* as it's rendered in postexilic Hebrew and Aramaic. In the Septuagint (the Greek translation of the Old Testament used in the first century), *Joshua* is regularly translated *Jesus* (*Iesous* in Greek). "Joshua" is the combination of two Hebrew words meaning "Yahweh saves." You may remember that Joshua in the Old Testament was originally "Hoshea," meaning "salvation," but Moses renamed him Joshua (Num. 13:16).

"Jesus," like its antecedent "Joshua," also means "Yahweh saves," or simply, "savior."

Although *Jesus* was a common name, with *Jesus of Nazareth* the name took on added significance. It didn't just mean that His God saves; it meant that He was the God who saves. Jesus of Nazareth is the only one who can save us from our sins. Salvation cannot be found in Muhammad or Krishna or a strong education or marriage or parents or children or presidents or prime ministers or millennial goals or any other name or thing that can be named under heaven (Acts 4:12).

And don't miss what should be obvious, that Jesus saves us from *our sins* (Matt. 1:21). The point of the gospel is not that Jesus saves us from low self-esteem, or from singleness, or from our crummy job. As evangelicals, we do better defending the truth that Jesus is our Savior than we do remembering what He actually saves us from. Sin is our deepest, most fundamental, most pervasive problem. Other teachers and heroes may be able to save us from life's stresses and disappointments, but with this problem of sin, there is only One who can save, and His name is Jesus.

Consequently, we must "not look for . . . salvation and security in saints." This is generally not a problem in Protestant churches. Praying to saints, hoping for the extra merit of saints, and keeping feasts days for the saints is a Roman Catholic phenomenon. These seem like obvious cultural accretions to most Protestants—after all there is only one mediator between God and men, the man Christ Jesus (1 Tim. 2:5). But this doesn't mean Protestants are off the hook. Are we not just as likely to feel "saved" because our parents are godly or our grandparents went to church every Sunday, or because we went to church when we were kids twenty years ago? But never forget: God has no grandchildren. We must each stand before Him with faith that is our own. Trusting in upbringing or parental involvement is looking for salvation and security in saints, not in Christ.

More convicting still is the next phrase in Question 30—"in themselves." Protestants don't pray to saints, but we sure work hard to do what is right. Deep down, and sometimes we don't even have to dig that deep, many of us feel confident before God because we haven't royally messed up our lives, at least not lately. We don't get drunk or do drugs. We show up on time for work. We keep our yard clean and get involved in church.

I'd feel pretty good with a record like that. I do feel pretty good sometimes! And that's my problem. I put my trust in Kevin. The fact that when I sin I feel like I should earn my repentance before I come back to God tells me that I live too much of my life feeling good with God because I feel like I am good enough for God. I don't need Pelagianism or semi-Pelagianism or liberalism or the power of positive thinking to make me full of myself. I was born full of myself, and every day needs to be emptied and filled with Christ.

There is nowhere else we ought to look for our salvation than in Christ. You cannot trust Christ truly unless you trust Christ alone. No matter how much you boast of Christ or talk of your love for Christ or passion for Christ, if you add anything to Christ, your boasting and love and passion are all in vain. There is no "both-and" with Jesus, only "either-or." *Either* Jesus is the only Savior, the perfect Savior, and your only comfort in life and in death, *or* Jesus is for you no Savior at all.

31. **Q.** WHY IS HE CALLED "CHRIST," MEANING "ANOINTED"?

A. Because He has been ordained by God the Father and has been anointed with the Holy Spirit to be our chief prophet and teacher who perfectly reveals to us the secret counsel and will of God for our deliverance; our only high priest who has set us free by the one sacrifice of His body, and who continually pleads our cause with the Father; and our eternal king who governs us by His Word and Spirit, and who guards us and keeps us in the freedom He has won for us.

32. **Q.** BUT WHY ARE YOU CALLED A CHRISTIAN?

A. Because by faith I am a member of Christ and so I share in His anointing. I am anointed to confess His name, to present myself to Him as a living sacrifice of thanks, to strive with a good conscience against sin and the devil in this life, and afterward to reign with Christ over all creation for all eternity.

The Christened One

*I*f Jesus was a common Jewish name in the first century, Christ certainly was not. In fact, Christ isn't even a name (as if Jesus inherited it from His parents, Joseph and Mary Christ). Christ is a title, or more accurately, *the* title. Many of us are so used to putting "Jesus" next to "Christ" that we scarcely know what we are saying. But first-century Jews would have known. "Christ" means anointed; it is simply the Greek equivalent of the Hebrew word "Messiah."

That's why there is so much discussion in the Gospels about "the Christ," where He comes from and what He is like and whose son He will be. Peter's confession, "You are the Christ, the Son of the living God" (Matt. 16:16), was so momentous because Peter was stating what was far from obvious to everyone else; namely, that this wonder-working son of a carpenter, this teacher who ate with sinners, this man who said such strange and powerful things, was the long-awaited Messiah—the bringer of a new kingdom, the deliverer of God's people, and the Savior of the world.

Jesus' mission was Trinitarian in nature. He was ordained by God the Father and anointed with the Holy Spirit as the Christ (Matt. 3:16–17). The three persons of the Trinity worked together in salvation as much as they did in creation. That's why notions of the cross as cosmic child abuse are terribly unhelpful and unhelpfully terrible. The Father is in the Son and the Son is in the Father. They are one (John 17:21–22). The death of the Son (the Spirit anointed Christ), who bore the wrath of God in place of sinners, is a testimony to the glory of Trinitarian love, fellowship, and unity, not the undermining of all these things.

Answer 31 goes on to explain that the Father ordained and the Spirit anointed Christ to fulfill three different offices: prophet, priest, and king. If you've ever struggled to explain Christ at the beach or around the water cooler, try using these three words. *Prophet, priest,* and *king* is not the only way to talk about Christ, but it has to be one of the simplest and best—better than contemporary ascriptions of Jesus as *revolutionary, homeboy,* or the *"center"* (never sure what to make of that one).

Christ is our chief prophet and teacher (Acts 3:22; Deut. 18:15). The word "chief" is important; it's what makes Christianity Christian. Muslims laud Jesus as a great prophet, but He is not the last and greatest prophet like Mohammed. Mormons worship Jesus as the Christ and the Son of God (understanding these words differently than Christians), but listen to Joseph Smith as the prophet we all must reckon with. Even many Jews will recognize Christ as a teacher sent by God, but not greater than Moses or Elijah and certainly not in fulfillment of Moses's and Elijah's ministries of lesser glory.

By contrast, for Christians Christ is our *chief* prophet, the one and only who makes known the Father (John 1:18) and reveals the exact nature of God (Heb. 1:3). As a prophet Christ came to show us the way and declare the will of God. But as the Messiah, our chief prophet, He came not just to reveal the will of God but to fulfill it, and He laid down His life, not just an example of the way *of* God but as the way *to* God.

Christ is also our only high priest (Heb. 7:17; Ps. 110:4). Again, the adjective is important. Christ is our *only* high priest. There's a reason Protestants have pastors or ministers instead of priests. It's because of a conviction—one most Protestants are unaware of—about the cessation of the official priesthood. The main role of the priest under the old covenant was to offer sacrifices to God, and once a year to enter the Holy of Holies on Yom Kippur and make atonement for the people. But according to the book of Hebrews, all that has ended. We need no more priests because we need no more sacrifices (Heb. 7:27; 9:12, 25–26; 10:10–18). The only priest we need is Jesus Christ because His sacrifice on the cross was the end of the sacrificial system. High priests served two related functions—making atonement and making intercession for the people—both of which are accomplished for us in Christ. Christ died for us (once for all, never to die again), and Christ prays for us (continually and repeatedly). This makes Him the greatest priest, the last priest, and the only priest we need.

Finally, Christ is our eternal king (Matt. 21:5; Zech. 9:9). As a king, Christ does two things: He governs and guards. The Catechism tells us Christ governs by Word and Spirit. Oh, how many theological stray cats have been sired by separating Word from Spirit. Word without Spirit is dead letter. Spirit without Word is hopeless relativism. Christ governs us by Word, to give us a propositional revelation of His will and an objective set of external truths, and by Spirit, to give us a subjective experience of His presence and the inner power to obey.

As king, Christ also guards. Kingship isn't all authority and fiats and gloomy threats. Good kings also protect their people. In this case, Christ keeps us—not happy, healthy, and wealthy—but free. He will not let us fall to the Devil (not ultimately), and He will not let us offer ourselves again to the world's bondage (not finally). He loves us and the freedom He purchased on our behalf.

One last note on the three offices of Christ: You'll notice that Q/A 32 uses the same sort of language to describe us as Christians. And as little Christs, ordained by the same Father and anointed by the same Spirit, we are to fulfill, in a lesser way, the same offices as our namesake. We confess His name like good prophets, present ourselves as living sacrifices like good priests, and fight our mutual enemies and reign in joint dominion like good kings. Remember this: The work of Christ and the life of a Christian can be summed up in three words: "prophet", "priest", and "king".

Lord's Day 13

33. Q. WHY IS HE CALLED GOD'S "ONLY SON" WHEN WE ALSO ARE GOD'S CHILDREN?

A. Because Christ alone is the eternal, natural Son of God. We, however, are adopted children of God—adopted by grace through Christ.

34. Q. WHY DO YOU CALL HIM "OUR LORD"?

A. Because—not with gold or silver, but with His precious blood—He has set us free from sin and the tyranny of the devil, and has bought us, body and soul, to be His very own.

His Son and Our Lord

*H*aving explained the words from the Apostles' Creed, "I believe in Jesus Christ," we now turn to an explanation of "His only Son, our Lord." Question 33 raises a question many of us have never considered. How can Jesus be God's *only* Son if we too are called sons (and daughters)? The answer lies in the distinction between natural children and adoption.

Because of Adam's sin, we are by nature children of wrath and sons of disobedience (Eph. 2:2–3). We are not born children of God as if it were our right as human beings. Rather, we must be made children of God by adoption. In the fullness of time, "God sent forth his Son, born of woman, born under the law, to redeem those who were under the law, so that we might receive adoption as sons" (Gal. 4:4–5).

J. I. Packer, author of the classic *Knowing God*, once summarized the gospel in just three words: "adoption through propitiation." Now, it strikes me as close to cheating when your simple summary uses two big Latinate words that beg for further explanation, but I have to hand it to Packer; his definition is elegantly profound. The short and sweet of the gospel is this: The wrath of God has been turned away from sinners because of the death of Christ so that we might be reconciled to God and brought into His family.

The Sonship of Jesus Christ, then, is different from ours in that we *became* children of God, whereas Jesus Christ has *always been* God's Son. Jesus was not made the Son of God at His incarnation as if some new title or identity was conferred upon Him. The Son of God was the Son of the Father even before creation (Heb. 1:2). His Sonship is eternal. Ours is not. That's the difference. By nature, we are not God's children, whereas Christ is by nature the Son of God.

But with all this talk of Jesus as the Son of God, we must not presume that God is a Father to the Son just as a man is a father to his son. There is, to put it theologically, no temporal filiation (i.e., begetting a son in time) in the Trinity. All of our sons became sons at their birth (technically at conception, I suppose), before which they did not exist. But the Son of God never came into being. He is God's eternally begotten Son. There never was a time when He was not. The Father did not give life to Him in the sense that He created the Son or brought the Son from nonbeing to being.

Rather, the Father shares His essence with the Son and the life He has in Himself (John 5:26). So for us, being called children of God means we have been given new life and graciously welcomed into the family of our heavenly Father. But for Jesus to be called God's only Son means that He shares equally in divinity, glory, and honor with the Father. Sometimes liberal theologians have argued that Jesus believed He was the Son of God in the same way that we are God's children, but this was plainly not the case. Even the Jews understood that when Jesus declared His radical unity with the Father as His only Son, He was daring to make Himself not just a spiritual child of God but equal to God Himself (John 5:18).

Perhaps we can understand Trinitarian orthodoxy by seeing what it is not. Mormons believe Jesus Christ is "Heavenly Father's Only Begotten Son in the flesh,"[15] which sounds like orthodox Christianity. But elsewhere they explain that Jesus "was born, as were all spirit children of the Father. God was His Father, as He is of all the rest."[16] Jesus was the firstborn spirit child of God and the recipient of the divine birthright. Jesus, in Mormon theology, is divine, but it is only a derivative divinity. He is not the natural Son of God, nor is His Sonship eternally and ontologically different than ours. Rather He inherited powers of Godhood and divinity from His Father, including immortality. As one Mormon theologian puts it, "He is God the Second, the Redeemer."[17] This is positively not what the Catechism, nor the ecumenical creeds, nor the Scriptures mean when they call Jesus Christ "God's only Son."

Jesus Christ is not only God's Son. He is our Lord. Christ has rights over us. Some of us have an entitlement complex. We think, "No one's the boss of me. I'm the master of my destiny. I'm the captain of my soul. I make the rules. I answer to no one." But as Christians, we know this spirit by another name—idolatry. Being a Christian means dying to ourselves and surrendering our rights to another. The rejection of Jesus Christ is sometimes an intellectual problem and sometimes an ignorance problem, but it is always a surrender problem. We don't easily submit ourselves to any authority, let alone One who claims dominion over every aspect of our lives. But Jesus has the right to be Lord over our rights.

Christ, according to Ursinus, can claim lordship over our lives for four reasons: by right of creation (He made us), by right of redemption (He saved us), by reason of preservation (He keeps us), and with respect to ordination and appointment (God has exalted Christ and placed all things in subjection under His feet). Christ's rule, then, is not some arbitrary authority by virtue of a military coup or political nepotism. His claim of lordship is well-founded.

Remember too, His lordship was also costly. Jesus Christ didn't establish His authority by taking prisoners, executing judgment, and shedding the blood of His enemies. He is Lord because He shed His own blood, bore God's judgment, and set the captives free. He purchased our bodies and souls with a commodity far more precious than stocks or bonds. He redeemed our lives by loving us enough to lose His own.

Lord's Day 14

35. Q. WHAT DOES IT MEAN THAT HE "WAS CONCEIVED BY THE HOLY SPIRIT AND BORN OF THE VIRGIN MARY"?

A. That the eternal Son of God, who is and remains true and eternal God, took to Himself, through the working of the Holy Spirit, from the flesh and blood of the virgin Mary, a truly human nature so that He might become David's true descendant, like His brothers in every way except for sin.

36. Q. HOW DOES THE HOLY CONCEPTION AND BIRTH OF CHRIST BENEFIT YOU?

A. He is our mediator, and with His innocence and perfect holiness He removes from God's sight my sin—mine since I was conceived.

Vital Virginity

The accounts of Jesus' birth in Matthew (chapter 1) and Luke (chapters 1–2) are clear and unequivocal: Jesus' birth was not ordinary. He was not an ordinary child and His conception did not come about in the ordinary way. His mother, Mary, was a virgin, having had no intercourse prior to conception. By the Holy Spirit, Mary's womb became the cradle of the Son's incarnation (Matt. 1:20; Luke 1:35).

It's no secret that in recent history, the doctrine of the virgin birth (or more precisely, the virginal conception) has been ridiculed as fairy-tale make-believe by many outside the church, and not a few voices inside the church. Two arguments are usually mentioned.

First, the prophecy about a virgin birth in Isaiah 7:14, it is argued, actually speaks of a young woman and not a virgin. (To be fair, some scholars make this argument about Isaiah's prophecy and still believe in the virgin birth.) Many have pointed out that the Hebrew word in Isaiah is *almah* and not the technical term for virgin, *bethula*. It is true that *almah* has a wider semantic range than *bethula*, but there are no clear references in the Old Testament where *almah* does not mean virgin. The word *almah* occurs nine times in the Old Testament, and wherever the context makes its meaning clear, the word refers to a virgin.

More importantly, the Septuagint (the Greek translation of the Hebrew Scriptures begun in the third century BC) translates *almah* with the Greek word *parthenos* (the same word used in Matt. 1:23 where Isa. 7:14 is quoted), and everyone agrees that *parthenos* means "virgin." The Jewish translators of the Septuagint would not have used a clear Greek word for virgin if they understood Isaiah 7:14 to refer to nothing more than a young woman.

Second, many have objected to the virgin birth because they see it as a fairly typical bit of pagan mythologizing. They argue, "Star Wars has a virgin birth. Mithraism had a virgin birth. Christianity has a virgin birth. Big deal. They are all just fables." This is a popular argument and it sounds quite plausible at first glance, but there are a number of problems with it.

1. The assumption that there was a prototypical God-man who had certain titles, did certain miracles, was born of a virgin, saved His people, and then got resurrected is not well founded. In fact, no such prototypical "hero" existed before the rise of Christianity.

2. It would have been unthinkable for a Jewish sect (which is what Christianity was initially) to try to win new converts by adding pagan elements to their gospel story. I suppose a good Jew might make up a story to fit the Old Testament, but to mix in bits of paganism would have been anathema to most Jews.

3. The virgin birth parallels are not as strong as we might think. Consider three of the usual suspects, Alexander the Great, Dionysus, and Mithra. *Alexander's* most reliable ancient biographer (several centuries after his death) makes no mention of a virgin birth. Besides, the story that began to circulate (after the rise of Christianity, it's worth mentioning) is about an unusual conception, but not a virgin birth (Alexander's parents were already married). *Dionysus* was born when a god (in this case Zeus) disguised himself as a human and impregnated a human princess. This is not a virgin birth and not like the Holy Spirit's role we read about in the Gospels. *Mithra*, a popular parallel was born of a rock, not a virgin. Moreover, the cult of Mithra in the Roman Empire dates to after the time of Christ so any dependence is Mithraism on Christianity and not the other way around.[18]

To the Greek warrior, the Greek god, and the cult of Mithra, we can add Buddha: His mother dreamed that Buddha entered her in the form of a white elephant. But this story doesn't appear until five centuries after his death and she was already married. You get the drift. The so-called parallels always occur well after the life in question, well into the Christian era, and are not really stories of virginal conceptions anyway.

But even for those who believe in the virgin birth, it is sometimes questioned whether the doctrine is really that important. For example, one pastor has argued, in what has become a very well-known passage, that the virgin birth may not be all that essential. "What if Jesus had an earthly father named Larry?" he asks. What if the virgin birth was thrown in to appeal to the followers of Mithra and Dionysian religious cults? What if the word for virgin referred to a woman who became pregnant the first time she had intercourse? He suggests that none of this would be catastrophic to the Christian faith. "What if that spring [the virgin birth] was seriously questioned? Could a person keep jumping? Could a person still love God? Could you still be a Christian? Is the way of Jesus still the best possible way to live?"[19]

There are a lot of questions here, but the underlying one seems to be this: Is the virgin birth really that essential to Christianity? The answer, the pastor's insinuation notwithstanding, is a resounding Yes!

First, the virgin birth is essential to Christianity because it has been essential to Christianity. That may sound like circular reasoning, but only if we care nothing about the history and catholicity of the church. Granted, the church can get things wrong, sometimes even for a long time. But if Christians, of all stripes in all places, have professed belief in the virgin birth for two millennia, maybe we should be slow to discount it as inconsequential. In his definitive study of the virgin birth, J. Gresham Machen concluded that "there can be no doubt that at the close of the second century the virgin birth of Christ was regarded as an absolutely essential part of the Christian belief by the Christian church in all parts of the known world."[20] Perhaps, then, we should not be so hasty in dismissing the doctrine as a take-it-or-leave-it element of the Christian faith.

Second, the gospel writers clearly believed that Mary was a virgin when Jesus was conceived. We don't know precisely how the Christ child came to be in Mary's womb, except that the conception was "from the Holy Spirit" (Matt. 1:20). But we do know that Mary understood the miraculous nature of this conception, having asked the angel "How will this be, since I am a virgin?" (Luke 1:34). The Gospels present the virgin birth as "an orderly account" of actual history from eyewitnesses (Luke 1:1–4).

If the virgin birth is false, the historical reliability of the Gospels is seriously undermined.

Third—and this intersects with the Catechism—the virgin birth demonstrates that Jesus was truly human and truly divine. How can the virgin birth be an inconsequential spring for our jumping when it establishes the very identity of our Lord and Savior? If Jesus had not been born of a human, we could not believe in His full humanity. But if His birth were like any other human birth—through the union of a human father and mother—we would question His full divinity. The virgin birth is necessary to secure both a real human nature and a completely divine nature.

Fourth, the virgin birth is essential because it means Jesus did not inherit the curse of depravity that clings to Adam's race. Jesus was made like us in every way except for sin (Heb. 4:15; 7:26–27). Every human father begets a son or daughter with his sin nature. We may not understand completely how this works, but this is the way of the world after the fall. Sinners beget sinners (Ps. 51:5). Always. So if Joseph was the real father of Jesus, or Mary had been sleeping around with Larry, Jesus is not spotless, not innocent, and not perfectly holy. And as a result, we have no mediator, no imputation of Christ's righteousness (because He has no righteousness to impute to us), and no salvation.

So, yeah, the virgin birth is essential to our faith.

*L*ord's Day 15

37. Q. WHAT DO YOU UNDERSTAND BY THE WORD "SUFFERED"?

A. That during His whole life on earth, but especially at the end, Christ sustained in body and soul the anger of God against the sin of the whole human race. This He did in order that, by His suffering as the only atoning sacrifice, He might set us free, body and soul, from eternal condemnation, and gain for us God's grace, righteousness, and eternal life.

38. Q. WHY DID HE SUFFER "UNDER PONTIUS PILATE" AS JUDGE?

A. So that He, though innocent, might be condemned by a civil judge, and so free us from the severe judgment of God that was to fall on us.

39. Q. IS IT SIGNIFICANT THAT HE WAS "CRUCIFIED" INSTEAD OF DYING SOME OTHER WAY?

A. Yes. This death convinces me that He shouldered the curse which lay on me, since death by crucifixion was accursed by God.

A Suffering Servant
for the Sheep

Womb to tomb, that's how quickly the Apostles' Creed covers the life of Jesus. It skips His public ministry and goes right from His birth to His death. The Creed does not make this leap to denigrate Jesus' teaching and miracles but because those who wrote the Creed, and the Catechism, not to mention Peter, John, and Paul in the Acts of the Apostles, understood that the main thing about Jesus' life was His death.

It should be obvious: The Gospels are mainly about the gospel. Already in Matthew 1 we read that Jesus will save His people from their sins. Already in John 1 we read that Jesus is the Lamb of God who takes away the sins of the world. Three times in Mark and three times in Luke, Jesus predicts His death prior to the Passion Week. Nine of the twenty-eight chapters in Matthew deal with the last week of Jesus' life—the events leading up to His execution, His death on a cross, and His resurrection from the dead. Passion Week accounts for six of Mark's sixteen chapters, six of Luke's twenty-four chapters, and nine of John's twenty-one chapters. So out of eighty-nine chapters in the four Gospels, thirty (one-third) are about the climatic final week of Jesus' life.

If we figure Jesus was thirty-three years old when He died, He lived around 1,700 weeks. And His four biographers spend a third of their time on only one of those weeks. Have you ever read a three-hundred-page biography where one hundred pages dealt with the subject's death? Not even for Abraham Lincoln, John Kennedy, or Martin Luther King Jr. do we have such lopsided attention paid to the end of the story. But for Jesus, the ending of His life is the story.

Yet, the Catechism makes clear that the ending of Jesus' life, with its severe affliction, was but an intensification of the entire life He lived. Although our pain-averse, comfort-prizing natures would like to forget it, we worship a Savior whose life was marked by profound suffering. Ursinus, Heidelberg's chief author, lists seven ways Christ suffered. (1) He gave up the joys of heaven. (2) He experienced the infirmities of our nature (hunger, thirst, sadness, grief, etc.). (3) He knew deprivation and poverty (i.e., He had nowhere to lay His head). (4) He endured insults, treacheries, slanders, blasphemies, rejection, and contempt. (5) He faced temptations from the Devil. (6) He died a shameful and painful death. (7) He experienced the bitter anguish of soul as one accursed of God and forsaken by His heavenly Father.[21]

This last point is especially important, because it reminds us that Jesus was not merely another tragic hero whose unjust punishment elicits our pity. As much as I was thankful for many aspects of Mel Gibson's *The Passion of the Christ*, I couldn't help but think that without a theological interpretation of Jesus' passion, most people watching the movie would end up simply feeling sorry for a good man who suffered so violently. But the scourge of whips and nail-marked hands doesn't begin to show us all that Christ suffered as He sustained, in body and soul, the anger of God against the sin of the human race. More than just another tragic human martyr, Jesus was the unique Son of God who suffered once for all for the sins of the world and shouldered, as no one else ever did, could, or will, the curse of God for us.

There is one more issue we need to touch on in this Lord's Day, the so-called L in TULIP—limited atonement. Did Jesus die for everyone or just for the elect? Answer 37 seems to go against Calvin and the Synod of Dort (1618–19) when it states that Christ sustained the anger of God "against the whole human race." Does this mean Jesus died for everyone? Sort of, but not in a way that undermines limited atonement. Ursinus explains in his commentary that Christ's death was for all "as it respects the sufficiency of satisfaction which He made, but not as it respects the application thereof."[22] In other words, the death of Christ was *sufficient* to atone for the sins of the whole world, but it was God's will that it should *effectively* redeem those and only those who were chosen from eternity to salvation and given to Christ by the Father.

Particular redemption is actually a more helpful term than *limited atonement*, because the point of the doctrine is not to limit the mercy of God, but to make clear that Jesus did not die in the place of every sinner on the earth, but for His particular people. The Good Shepherd lays His life down for the sheep (John 10:11). This is why John 6:37 says Jesus came to save those the Father had given to Him, and why Matthew 1:21 says He died for His people, and John 15:13 says for His friends, and Acts 20:28 says for the church, and Ephesians 5:25 says for His bride, and Ephesians 1:4 says for those chosen in Christ Jesus.

Some may argue that spending time on this doctrinal controversy is a waste of time, but the doctrine of particular redemption is worth talking about because it gets to the heart of the gospel. Should we say "Christ died so that sinners might come to him"? Or, "Christ died for sinners"? There's a big difference. Did Christ's work on the cross make it possible for sinners to come to God? Or did Christ's work on the cross actually reconcile sinners to God? In other words, does the death of Jesus Christ make us saveable or does it make us saved? If the atonement is not particularly and only for the sheep, then either we have universalism—Christ died in everyone's place and therefore everyone is saved—or we have something less than full substitution. If Jesus died for every person on the planet, then we no longer mean that He died in place of sinners, taking upon Himself our shame, our sins, and our rebellion so that we have the death of death in the death of Christ. Rather, we mean that when Jesus died He made it *possible* to come to Him if we will do our part and come to Him. But this is only half a gospel. Certainly, we need to come to Christ in faith. But faith is not the last work that finally makes us saved. Faith is trusting that Jesus has in fact died in our place and bore the curse for us—effectually, particularly, and perfectly.

Reformed people talk of "limited" atonement not because they have an interest in limiting the power of the cross, but in order to safeguard the central affirmation of the gospel that Christ is a Redeemer who really redeems. "We are often told that we limit the atonement of Christ," Spurgeon observed, "because we say that Christ has not made a satisfaction for all men, or all men would be saved." But, Spurgeon argues, it is the view of the atonement that says no one in particular was saved at the cross that actually limits Christ's death. "We say Christ so died that He infallibly secured the salvation of a multitude that no man can number who through Christ's death not only may be saved, but are saved, must be saved and cannot by any possibility run the hazard of being anything but saved."[23]

I belabor this point not to belittle Arminian brothers and sisters but to give Jesus Christ His full glory. Christ does not come to us merely saying, "I've done My part. I laid down My life for everyone because I have saving love for everyone in the whole world. Now, if you would only believe and come to Me, I can save you." Instead He says to us, "I was pierced for your transgressions. I was crushed for your iniquities. I have purchased with My blood people for God from every tribe and language and people and nation (see Isa. 53:5; Rev. 5:9). I Myself bore your sins in My body on the tree, so that you might infallibly die to sins and assuredly live for righteousness. For My wounds did not merely make healing available. They healed you" (see 1 Peter 2:24).

"Amazing love!" a great Arminian once wrote. "How can it be that You, my Lord, should die for me?!" Praise be to our Good Shepherd who didn't just make our salvation possible but sustained the anger of God in body and soul, shouldered the curse, and laid down His life for the sheep.

*L*ord's Day 16

40. Q. WHY DID CHRIST HAVE TO GO ALL THE WAY TO DEATH?

A. Because God's justice and truth demand it: only the death of God's Son could pay for our sin.

41. Q. WHY WAS HE "BURIED"?

A. His burial testifies that He really died.

42. Q. SINCE CHRIST HAS DIED FOR US, WHY DO WE STILL HAVE TO DIE?

A. Our death does not pay the debt for our sins. Rather, it puts an end to our sinning and is our entrance into eternal life.

43. Q. WHAT FURTHER ADVANTAGE DO WE RECEIVE FROM CHRIST'S SACRIFICE AND DEATH ON THE CROSS?

A. Through Christ's death our old selves are crucified, put to death, and buried with Him, so that the evil desires of the flesh may no longer rule us, but that instead we may dedicate ourselves as an offering of gratitude to Him.

44. Q. WHY DOES THE CREED ADD, "HE DESCENDED TO HELL"?

A. To assure me in times of personal crisis and temptation that Christ my Lord, by suffering unspeakable anguish, pain, and terror of soul, especially on the cross but also earlier, has delivered me from the anguish and torment of hell.

Death and Hell

*J*esus Christ died for our sins. God's justice demanded it, and His burial testifies to it. Jesus did not swoon or slip into a coma or fall asleep on the cross. He died—stone-cold dead and buried.

But why then do we still die? If Christ's death meant the death of death and paid in full the penalty for our sin, why do one hundred out of one hundred Christians still die?

Death is our entrance into eternal life. We know that. But have you ever stopped to think that death also puts an end to our sinning? I don't think I've ever comforted the dying with this thought. But I should. When a loved one dies of cancer or some debilitating disease, we often hear how "they fought bravely for many years, and now the fight is over and her suffering has ended." We ought to say the same thing about spiritual disease: "She loved the Lord with all her heart and fought against indwelling sin for the past forty years. Now the fight is over and she has overcome."

Granted, there are aspects of dying that frighten us. But the Catechism reminds us of an aspect of the good news that we often forget. After death, we won't think another proud thought, we won't snap at our children again, we won't face another temptation to lust ever again. What sweet relief.

Christ's death not only pays for our sins and assures us of sinless eternal life, it also means that our sinful natures have been put to death in this life. Progressive sanctification is built on the atonement. We have been crucified with Christ. We have been buried with Him. We died to sin in His death. This doesn't mean the fight for holiness is over but rather that the fight can now begin. It is only Christ's finished work on the cross that frees us and inspires us to a life of good works, piety, and gratitude.

But what about this business in the Creed about Christ descending into hell? What are we to do with this strange phrase? One option, an option I can respect, is to dump it altogether. The phrase "descended into hell" has been found in only one version of the Creed prior to AD 650, and in that instance the phrase was understood to mean "descended into the grave." So, historically, there is some question about whether "descended into hell" should even be a part of the Creed.

But considering the phrase has been a part of the Apostles' Creed for at least 1,300 years, we should not dismiss it lightly. But we need to understand the phrase biblically if we are going to keep saying it. There are three ways to understand "descended into hell." The phrase could refer to death. This is how Rufinus understood it with his version of the Creed in AD 390. The Greek word *hades* in Rufinus's version can simply mean the grave (*gehenna* being the more technical term for hell as a place of punishment). The problem with this view is that it makes the phrase redundant. Why do we need to confess that Jesus descended to the grave when the Creed already states that He died and was buried?

Another option is to take "hell" as the place of eternal punishment. Jesus, on this understanding, spent the days between His death and resurrection in the place of eternal torment with the damned. This interpretation has many problems. For starters, Jesus told the thief on the cross they would be together that very day in paradise (Luke 23:43), a promise made difficult to deliver on if Jesus was on His way to hell. Plus, it's hard to imagine Jesus crying out "It is finished" (John 19:30) and "Into your hands I commit my spirit" (Luke 23:46), if He had more suffering to endure in hell.

Moreover, the passages trotted out to defend Christ's descent into a literal hell are unconvincing. Ephesians 4:9 speaks of Christ descending into the lower parts of the earth, but the reference here is to the incarnation. First Peter 4:6 says the gospel was preached even to those who are dead, but this is simply a reference to those who are now dead, not to the dead receiving preaching while in hell. Related to this is the confusing passage in 1 Peter 3 about Christ preaching to the spirits in prison (vv. 18–20). This seems like the medieval "harrowing of hell" where Jesus goes to the netherworld and tries to rescue the condemned. But the context has to do with the disobedient of Noah's generation. The point of the passage is that the Spirit of Christ (1:11) was preaching through Noah (cf. 2 Peter 2:5) as he warned the ungodly souls before the flood who are now imprisoned under God's judgment. In other words, the text is about God speaking through Noah to the disobedient in his generation, not Christ going to hell after death to save them then.

This leaves us with a final option, the one we find in Answer 44. Christ's descent into hell is to be understood spiritually. To be honest, I'm not sure if this captures the original intent behind the phrase, if we can even be certain of the original intent, but a spiritual understanding of Christ's hell makes the most sense in the light of Scripture and allows me to confess the Creed in good conscience. Jesus "descended into hell" as He suffered the pain and torment of divine wrath. "Surely no more terrible abyss can be conceived," writes Calvin, "than to feel yourself forsaken and estranged from God; and when you call upon him not to be heard."[24] It should be a comfort to us in our torment that there is no hell we can face greater than the one Christ endured; that there is no one better to sympathize with our hellish moments than Christ; and that there is no one else able to save us from the wrath of God than He who has faced it already.

45. Q. HOW DOES CHRIST'S RESURRECTION BENEFIT US?

A. First, by His resurrection He has overcome death, so that He might make us share in the righteousness He won for us by His death. Second, by His power we too are already now resurrected to a new life. Third, Christ's resurrection is a guarantee of our glorious resurrection.

The Resurrection's Relevance

There has been no more important event in history than the resurrection of the Son of God. And don't overlook the word *history* in that last sentence. Christianity is an historical religion. We believe and proclaim certain events that happened—really happened, as everyone except madmen and New Testament scholars understand things to have really happened. Easter is not about Jesus living on in His teachings or the experience of Jesus coming to life in His disciples. Easter is about a divine Galilean whose heart pumped blood again, whose lungs filled with oxygen again, and whose synapses started firing again.

"What was it that within a few days transformed a band of mourners into the spiritual conquerors of the world?" asked J. Gresham Machen. "It was not the memory of Jesus' life; it was not the inspiration which came from past contact with Him. But it was the message, 'He is risen.' That message alone gave to the disciples a living Saviour; and it alone can give to us a living Saviour today."[25] If the historical Jesus is something other than the Jesus who died for sins, was buried, and raised to life again, then He was a failure and a fraud and we are mistaken in our devotion to Him.

Rewriting history is a problem for some, but the bigger problem for most churchgoers is ignorance about the implications of the resurrection. Most of us can jubilantly sing *Christ the Lord Is Risen Today* without crossing our fingers or resorting to metaphors in our minds, but many haven't given much thought as to why this is such good news, other than that Jesus lives and as a general rule we like the idea of good people not staying dead. Sometimes this ignorance is the fault of preachers who spend so much time defending the resurrection against skeptics and naysayers that they do little to exult in the benefits that are ours through our once-dead-but-now-alive Lord. Answer 45 gives three succinct reasons why the resurrection of the Son of God is good news for us.

First, by His resurrection Jesus Christ has overcome death, so that He might make us share in the righteousness He won for us by His death. First Corinthians 15 makes it clear that if Jesus has not been raised, our "faith is futile" and we "are still in [our] sins" (v. 17). Why is the resurrection, and not simply the cross alone, necessary for the forgiveness of sin? Because without the resurrection nothing has been conquered—not sin, not death, not the Devil. Jesus' resurrection from the dead testifies not only that Jesus is the Son of God (Rom. 1:4) but that the offering of life was an acceptable sacrifice to God. If Jesus had not been raised, it would be an indication to us that the work of salvation had not yet been accomplished.

Conversely, His being raised indicates the satisfaction of divine justice. The punishment is over. The merit of Christ has proven worthy. The debt has been paid. Death has been vanquished. Sin has been atoned for.

Imagine you are one of six boys in your family. One day, five of you sneak out of your rooms, ride your bikes to the grocery store, steal fireworks and lighters, come home and start blowing stuff up in your driveway. Being naughty and not very bright young boys, you light the firecrackers with Mom and Dad just inside the house. Soon the parental units are both outside and the five of you are in big trouble. But just then, your older brother, who has been learning about sine and cosine in his room, comes to your defense and offers to be punished in your place, even though he had no part in your crime. So Mom and Dad send him to his room and make clear that though the five of you are guilty and your older brother is innocent, he will pay for your sin and merit your forgiveness by going to his room.

Now as long as big brother is in his room, you feel as though you are not yet cleared for your crime. Until the door opens and your big brother emerges, you sense that the punishment is still being meted out. You don't know if this little switcheroo is actually going to work. But once big brother is set free, you rejoice, because now you know your penalty has been paid and Mom and Dad have nothing against you. The empty room indicates the satisfaction of parental justice.

The resurrection means the death of Jesus was enough—enough to atone for sin, enough to reconcile us to God, enough to present us holy in God's presence. Christ won; sin, death, and the Devil lost—that's the good news of the empty tomb. The resurrection means Christ proved Himself righteous to the Father, so that through faith we now can share in His righteousness.

Second, by Christ's power we too are already now resurrected to a new life. Our hope of new life is not just a future goal; it is a present reality. Dozens of times in the New Testament we see the phrase "in Christ." This little phrase speaks to the glorious union believers have with Christ through faith. We died in His death and we rose again in His resurrection to new life (Rom. 6:5–11; Eph. 2:5). But this new life is not as good as it's going to get.

The third benefit of Christ's resurrection is that it guarantees our future glorious resurrection. Christ's resurrection was the firstfruits of a resurrection harvest yet to come (1 Cor. 15:23). It's not hard to imagine women, like those racing from the empty tomb to tell the disciples He is no longer dead, coming in from the fields with the good news that the first ear of ripe corn had just been plucked and the rest of the splendid harvest is not far behind. Easter confirms that we have new bodies coming. No one knows exactly how God will gather our molecules from the sea and the ground, but He will put us back together again, in some ways just like we are, but in all ways new and better. Therefore, "we await a Savior, the Lord Jesus Christ, who will transform our lowly body to be like his glorious body" (Phil. 3:20–21).

46. Q. WHAT DO YOU MEAN BY SAYING, "HE ASCENDED TO HEAVEN"?

A. That Christ, while His disciples watched, was lifted up from the earth to heaven and will be there for our good until He comes again to judge the living and the dead.

47. Q. BUT ISN'T CHRIST WITH US UNTIL THE END OF THE WORLD AS HE PROMISED US?

A. Christ is truly human and truly God. In His human nature Christ is not now on earth; but in His divinity, majesty, grace, and Spirit He is not absent from us for a moment.

48. Q. IF HIS HUMANITY IS NOT PRESENT WHEREVER HIS DIVINITY IS, THEN AREN'T THE TWO NATURES OF CHRIST SEPARATED FROM EACH OTHER?

A. Certainly not. Since divinity is not limited and is present everywhere, it is evident that Christ's divinity is surely beyond the bounds of the humanity He has taken on, but at the same time His divinity is in and remains personally united to His humanity.

49. Q. HOW DOES CHRIST'S ASCENSION TO HEAVEN BENEFIT US?

A. First, He pleads our cause in heaven in the presence of His Father. Second, we have our own flesh in heaven—a guarantee that Christ our head will take us, His members, to Himself in heaven. Third, He sends His Spirit to us on earth as a further guarantee. By the Spirit's power we make the goal of our lives, not earthly things, but the things above where Christ is, sitting at God's right hand.

The Forgotten Ending

*I*s there any part of Christ's life that we think about less than His ascension? Everyone knows about His birth—that's what Christmas is for. His death, burial, and resurrection are pretty well covered by Holy Week. But who notices Ascension Day each spring? Of course, we remember that Jesus floated into heaven or some weird thing like that, but it's not really the sort of thing we meditate on in the wee hours of the night or share with Grandma before heart surgery. Ascension is simply the way Jesus checked out of planet Earth—that's all there is to it. Right?

But like every phrase in the Apostles' Creed, "He ascended to heaven" is confessed for a reason. As we'll see in a moment, Christ's ascension benefits us in several ways. But before we get there, we have this tricky business about the two natures of Christ.

Christ's human nature is not now on earth. We can't see Jesus face-to-face, go shake His hand, or hear Him preach on a hillside. Jesus Christ, the God-Man (still fully God *and* fully man) is in heaven, sitting at the right hand of God the Father. Contrary to the Lutheran idea of the "ubiquity" of the body of Christ (which is why Lutherans believe in a real "physical" presence in Communion), the Heidelberg Catechism teaches, rightly I believe, that Christ's body, being a real human body with limitations of time and space, can only be in one place at one time—and that place is heaven.

The divine nature, however, is not limited to one location. This doesn't mean Jesus is split in two with His humanity in heaven and His divinity flying around the planet incognito. The two natures are still joined and cannot be separated. The hypostatic union of the two natures resides in heaven. But how can Christ be everywhere then? The answer lies in the mystery of the Trinity. The Holy Spirit is the Spirit of Christ (Rom. 8:9), proceeding from the Father and the Son (John 15:26, Nicene Creed). So where the Spirit is, there the Son is also. The three persons of the Trinity experience fellowship among themselves in the dance (*perichoresis*) of mutual indwelling, so that, though they are distinct persons, it can rightly be said that if you've seen the Son, you've seen the Father, and if you have the Spirit, you have the Son. By His Spirit, then, Christ is not absent from us for a moment, though, in one sense, He has gone to "live" in heaven.

So how does Christ's ascension benefit us? In three ways. First, Christ's ascension benefits us because we have an advocate with the Father, Jesus Christ the righteous (1 John 2:1). Our Lord Jesus is in heaven pleading our case, so that whenever Satan accuses us in our conscience or dares to lay a charge against us before the Father, Jesus Christ, God's own Son and our flawless advocate, stands ready to defend us and plead His own blood for our sakes. Think about that. Christ is our prayer partner in heaven. He intercedes for us before the throne (Rom. 8:34).

Second, Christ's ascension benefits us because we now have our own flesh in heaven; our lives are hidden with Christ who dwells in glory above (Col. 3:3–4). Christ's flesh in heaven is a guarantee that ours will be there too someday. Our hope is not an eternity as disembodied souls but real, resurrected, material human bodies in God's presence forever. Christ's body is the first one there, but not the last.

Third, Christ's ascension benefits us because we get the Holy Spirit as a result. As Jesus Himself explained to His disciples, "It is to your advantage that I go away, for if I do not go away, the Helper will not come to you. But if I go, I will send him to you" (John 16:7). This was no knock on His own earthly ministry, but Jesus understood that as a man He was limited to one place at a time. But once He ascended to heaven, He could send another Helper (John 14:16) to give us power from on high and to be with us forever.

You may not think about the ascension again for quite some time, so mediate on this doctrine with me for two more minutes. Think about the implications of Christ's ascension. The ascension means we are in heaven, right now. Through union with Christ, we truly are not citizens of this world. Colossians tells us to set our minds on things that are above, because our lives are hidden with Christ who dwells there (3:2–3).

The ascension also implies that "asking Jesus into your heart" does not mean inviting a kind friend or comforting therapist into your life. It means—if we are using the nonbiblical phrase in a biblical way—that we are expressing our desire to be one with the king of the universe. The Jesus who lives within our hearts is sitting exalted at the right hand of God the Father Almighty.

Most staggering of all, the ascension means that God has granted all rule, power, authority, and dominion (Eph. 1:21–22) to a man! Maybe this is why Tolkien made such a point in *The Lord of the Rings* to emphasize that a man would sit on Gondor's throne, and the race of men would reign once more. Jesus Christ is exercising the dominion that man was made to have from the very beginning (Gen. 1:28). Because of Christ's ascension, we know that the incarnation continues, Christ's humanity lives on in heaven, the Spirit lives in our hearts, and a fleshy, divine human being rules the universe.

50. Q. WHY THE NEXT WORDS: "AND IS SEATED AT THE RIGHT HAND OF GOD"?

A. Christ ascended to heaven, there to show that He is head of His church, and that the Father rules all things through Him.

51. Q. HOW DOES THIS GLORY OF CHRIST OUR HEAD BENEFIT US?

A. First, through His Holy Spirit He pours out His gifts from heaven upon us His members. Second, by His power He defends us and keeps us safe from all enemies.

52. Q. HOW DOES CHRIST'S RETURN "TO JUDGE THE LIVING AND THE DEAD" COMFORT YOU?

A. In all my distress and persecution I turn my eyes to the heavens and confidently await as judge the very One who has already stood trial in my place before God and so has removed the whole curse from me. All His enemies and mine He will condemn to everlasting punishment: but me and all His chosen ones He will take along with Him into the joy and the glory of heaven.

The Return of the King

*H*ebrews 1 tells us that after making purification for sins, Jesus "sat down at the right hand of the Majesty on high, having become as much superior to angels as the name he has inherited is more excellent than theirs" (vv.3–4). It's striking imagery if you think about it. Picture an attorney making his closing arguments to the jury, and then after a crescendo of rhetoric, he says, "I rest my case" and sits back down next to his notes.

Or think of a mom who has had no time for herself all day. She's made meals, cleaned the house, changed diapers, folded clothes, helped with homework, played in the backyard, raced to the grocery store, and now finally has the kids snoozing in their beds. She walks wearily down the stairs and for the first time since she woke up fourteen hours ago, she sits down.

In both examples, sitting down is more than an act of rest. It is representative of completion. All that was necessary has been accomplished.

That's why it's thrilling to think that Jesus is *seated* at the right hand of God. His work is finished. He accomplished all that was needful for our salvation. And having shown Himself to be the victor over sin, death, and the Devil, it is given to Him to sit, not in any old place but at the place of honor and exaltation at God's right hand. All things have been placed under His feet (Eph. 1:20–22). All authority in heaven and on earth has been given to Him (Matt. 28:18).

The last line of the "Jesus" section of the Apostles' Creed confesses that Christ is coming again "to judge the living and the dead." The Catechism, in keeping with its overall theme, asks "How does Christ's return . . . *comfort* you?" That's a good question, because most of us don't think about coming judgment as an unspeakable comfort. But for those whose only comfort in life and in death is that they are not their own but belong body and soul to their faithful Savior, Jesus Christ, His return is their blessed hope (Titus 2:13).

The second coming comforts the believer in at least three ways. First, Christ's return means full and public acquittal for His people. I love the way the Catechism puts it: "I turn my eyes to the heavens and confidently await as judge the very One who has already stood trial in my place before God and so has removed the whole curse from me." We don't have to fear standing trial, because the judge has already stood trial in our place. Though we are guilty as sin (literally), there is no sentence left to be handed down. When you stand before the holy Son of God at the end of the age and all your deeds and thoughts are laid bare for the world to see—all your petty jealousies, all your lustful glances, all your murderous thoughts, all your self-absorbed days—there will still be nothing to fear. There is no chance that Christ will look you up and down and cry out "Curse this one!" because He already became the curse for us. We can no more be condemned at the throne of God's judgment than God can condemn Himself a second time.

The return of Christ also means vindication for God's people. All Christ's enemies and ours—our *real* enemies who oppose us because they oppose the gospel, not the "enemies" we can't get along with or hate without cause—will be condemned to everlasting punishment. Hell is the place where the worm never dies (Isa. 66:24), the fire is never quenched (Mark 9:48), and the smoke of their torment never ceases (Rev. 14:11).

But how, you ask, is this any sort of comfort? It's a comfort because God's name will be vindicated and the injustices against God and His people will finally be dealt with. Before we throw out the doctrine of hell, we should consider the possibility that it is offensive to us because we have no real enemies, have not suffered much at the hands of others, and our faith has cost us little. "O Sovereign Lord, holy and true, how long before You will judge and avenge our blood on those who dwell on the earth?" rings hollow when your "enemies" are an overbearing mother-in-law and "the drive-by media." The cry sounds more palatable when your enemies are people with swords killing you and your family for being Christians (Rev. 6:10). When the whole world wrongly hates you for being a Christian, the return of the righteous judge is unspeakable comfort.

Third, the return of Christ means that we will dwell with Christ body and soul in the glory of heaven. The coming of the judge means the coming of the end—the end of suffering, the end of depression, the end of cancer, the end of loneliness, and the end of sinning. Christ's return also means a beginning—the beginning of ceaseless praise, the beginning of perfect communion with God, and the beginning of delight that increases forever. In short, the beginning of the joyful end that never ends.

*L*ord's Day 20

53. Q. WHAT DO YOU BELIEVE CONCERNING "THE HOLY SPIRIT"?

A. First, He, as well as the Father and the Son, is eternal God. Second, He has been given to me personally, so that, by true faith, He makes me share in Christ and all His blessings, comforts me, and remains with me forever.

The Divine, Comforting, Always and Forever Holy Spirit

*M*any Christians rarely think about the Holy Spirit. God the Father we know about. God the Son we think about all the time. But God the Holy Spirit? It is often true: Traditional conservative Christians know too little about, and cherish too lightly, the person and work of the Holy Spirit. But before we pursue this criticism too far, we need to remember that the New Testament itself says a great deal more about Jesus Christ and God the Father than it does about the Spirit.

More importantly, we must not forget that the work of the Holy Spirit is first of all to glorify Christ (John 16:14). So whether we realize it or not, we are very intimately connected with the work of the Spirit, because wherever we are drawn to Christ as Savior, led to worship Christ as Lord, made to behold Christ as glorious, we are being operated on by the Holy Spirit.

The focus of most of our churches (like the Creed and the Catechism) is on Christ and not the Spirit, because that's the focus of the apostolic gospel, the New Testament, and the Holy Spirit Himself! Of course, this is not to suggest that singing to the Holy Spirit or worshiping Him is inappropriate. Far from it. Every person of the Trinity is equally glorious and deserving of praise. But Spirit-led worship has at its heart not an emotive experience (though emotions are good), nor a spontaneous feel (though spontaneity isn't bad), but rather a Christ-exalting, cross-focused, Word-centered event where the name of

Jesus is praised in the power of the Spirit to the glory of God the Father.

Answer 53 outlines the doctrine of the Holy Spirit using two broad categories: the person and the work of the Spirit. Remember, *the Holy Spirit is a person*—a teaching (Luke 12:11–12), speaking (Acts 13:2), interceding (Rom. 8:26), grieving (Eph. 4:30) person—distinct from the Father and the Son. The Holy Spirit is not a force or a principle of nature or a mode of God's existence. The Spirit is eternal God.

He is everywhere, which does not mean the Spirit is everything or in everything, but rather that there is nowhere we can go where the Spirit isn't also present (Ps. 139:7). The Spirit is eternal (Heb. 9:14). The Spirit alone knows the mind of God (1 Cor. 2:10–11). The Holy Spirit is fully divine, His name being used interchangeably with the name "God" (see Acts 5:3–4, where lying to God and lying to the Holy Spirit are equated, and 1 Corinthians 3:16 and 6:19, where the temple of God and the temple of the Holy Spirit are used synonymously). The Holy Spirit is active in our salvation along with the Father and the Son (1 Peter 1:1–2). Jesus commands His disciples to be baptized in the name (singular) of all three persons (plural) of the Trinity, underlying the equality of rank, power, and majesty among Father, Son, and Holy Spirit, while also emphasizing their fundamental unity (Matt. 28:19; cf. 2 Cor. 13:14).

The second category concerns the *work of the Holy Spirit*. The first thing the Catechism notes here is that the Holy Spirit "has been given to me personally." The Holy Spirit is not simply an omnipresent being who is with us in the sense that He is everywhere and so wherever we go there He will be also. The Spirit lives within us (1 Cor. 6:19) and makes His dwelling in our hearts (2 Cor. 1:22; Gal. 4:6). We have fellowship with Him (2 Cor. 13:14). This physical imagery should not be understood spatially as if the Spirit gets His mail delivered in the upper left chamber of that beating muscle in the chest. Rather, the Spirit dwells in us by animating our personality, shaping our character, renewing our mind, and stirring our emotions. His presence is not a physical residence as much as an experienced reality.

The Catechism goes on to mention three benefits we experience through the work of the Holy Spirit. (Note: The words "by faith" in the Catechism are important. The Spirit does not work to make anonymous Christians who have the blessings of Christ apart from belief in Christ. The benefits are only ours by faith. It is by trusting in Christ, resting in Christ, and depending solely on Christ that the Holy Spirit works in us.) The first benefit is that we share in Christ and all His blessings. Surely if anyone is blessed of God, it is His Son. And by the Spirit, we too now share in all His blessings. We too are looked on with favor. Everything Christ accomplished is ours. All He won is ours. The promised inheritance of Abraham is ours (Gal. 3:14). All this and more because we belong to Christ and Christ's blessings belong to us through ministrations of the Spirit.

The second benefit is the Holy Spirit's comfort. Most of us have heard that the Holy Spirit is a Comforter (John 14:16 KJV). Other translations render *paracletos* a "Helper" (ESV), a "Counselor" (NIV), or an "Advocate" (NRSV), but the truth is still there: God comforts His people by the Holy Spirit. This happens in a number of ways. The Spirit may supernaturally strengthen your soul and give you a peace that passes understanding or a calm confidence in the work of the Lord (Acts 9:31). He may also comfort you through other Christians as you share in the fellowship of the Holy Spirit. As the Spirit of truth, He will often speak to you through the Word of God, leading you into all truth (John 16:13), encouraging you with the words of Scripture He inspired and now illuminates. He may cause you to remember a precious biblical truth or direct your thoughts to the finished work of Christ or give you eyes to see more clearly the glory of God.

The third benefit is the Holy Spirit's presence forever. In heaven, the Spirit will continue to teach us more about the inexhaustible riches of Christ. He will continue to be the personal bond that unites believers in fellowship. And He will continue to minister to us the presence of God the Father and God the Son, who together with the Holy Spirit are triune God, blessed forevermore, amen.

54. Q. WHAT DO YOU BELIEVE CONCERNING "THE HOLY CATHOLIC CHURCH"?

A. I believe that the Son of God through His Spirit and Word, out of the entire human race, from the beginning of the world to its end, gathers, protects, and preserves for Himself a community chosen for eternal life and united in true faith. And of this community I am and always will be a living member.

55. Q. WHAT DO YOU UNDERSTAND BY "THE COMMUNION OF SAINTS"?

A. First, that believers one and all, as members of this community, share in Christ and in all His treasures and gifts. Second, that each member should consider it a duty to use these gifts readily and cheerfully for the service and enrichment of the other members.

56. Q. WHAT DO YOU BELIEVE CONCERNING "THE FORGIVE-NESS OF SINS"?

A. I believe that God, because of Christ's atonement, will never hold against me any of my sins nor my sinful nature which I need to struggle against all my life. Rather, in His grace God grants me the righteousness of Christ to free me forever from judgment.

The Church of the Reckoned Righteous

A couple of summers ago, I read through a whole stack of books about why the church is lame. True at times, but the church, we must not forget, was Christ's idea (Matt. 16:18), not to mention His bride (Eph. 5:25–33). There is no New Testament evidence of churchless Christians. New converts in the early church were baptized in Christ *and* into a body. Acts tells us the Lord added daily to their number those who were being saved (2:47). The Lord wasn't saving random people into individual saving relationships. He was adding people to the already visible, identifiable body of Christ.

Perhaps we would be less likely to overlook the importance of the church if we paid more attention to the Apostles' Creed. After all, almost every Christian agrees the Creed is a good summary of the essentials of the faith, and the Creed has us confess: "I believe in God the Father. I believe in Jesus Christ His only Son. I believe in the Holy Spirit. I believe in the church." If three of those matter, the fourth ought to too.

The Greek word for church is *ekklesia*, which means "gathering" or "assembly," coming from two Greek words meaning "called out ones." The simplest definition of the church is a community of persons called by God through His Word and Spirit to be His people (Answer 54). More specifically, theologians often speak of the church in terms of catholicity, apostolicity, and unity. We believe in the catholic, or universal, church, a community not defined by culture or race but by one Lord and one baptism. We believe in the apostolic church, an institution built on the foundation of the doctrine of the apostles. And we believe in a united church, a group of diverse people and local expressions sharing, not simply a slogan or a religious experience but one true faith. As believers we belong to this holy church, owe to her our allegiance, and as part of this body owe each other our love and service.

We've already read about the substitutionary atonement, God's grace for sinners, and salvation from coming judgment. All of this is summarized again in Answer 56. But notice two other points. First, the catechism is decidedly not perfectionistic. There is no illusion that the Christian will overcome outward and inward sin. There is no false assurance that we are going to go weeks or days (or even hours) without anger creeping into our souls, or lust stealing away our thoughts, our pride trying to usurp our hearts. On the contrary, I will struggle against my sinful nature all my life.

This means I can't automatically assume that the desires I have as a Christian are pure and pleasing to God. Sometimes you hear people say that sort of thing. "I am a new creation. God has given me a new heart. My desires are not suspect; they are from God Himself." This kind of thinking grossly underestimates the power of remaining sin in our lives. The mortification of the flesh is not a onetime event but an ongoing process. Each morning there are new temptations to avoid and more works of the flesh to put to death.

But, strangely, I find this more encouraging than discouraging. If the Lord gives me another thirty years, I will wake up as a sixty-year-old and still be frustrated by myself. I can count on it. I will not be completely sanctified. There will be growth and maturity, I hope, but not perfection. I will still be struggling with my self-centeredness, impatience, and indifference to so much of God's glory. And because of Christ's blood, God will still not hold these sins against me. This is not an excuse for laziness in the war against sin, but it is a call for perpetual joy and gratitude at the forgiveness that is mine through no work of my own.

The second thing to notice is that Answer 56 makes explicit the doctrine of the imputation of Christ's righteousness. Christ not only died the shameful death we deserved. He also lived the perfect life we could not. There has been a great exchange: my sin for His righteousness. I love the words written by the great Presbyterian churchman and theologian J. Gresham Machen just before he died on New Year's Day 1936. Alone in a

North Dakota hospital, he wrote to a friend and colleague: "I am so thankful for the active obedience of Christ. No hope without it."[26] Most of us have never heard of the "active obedience of Christ," let alone would we think to use the phrase for our last recorded words on earth. Theologians call the perfect life of Jesus His "active obedience" and Jesus' willingness to die His "passive obedience." So Machen's dying hope was that Christ had lived the perfect life for his sake. He was confident not only that the death of Jesus made him innocent before God but that the life of Jesus made him positively righteous.

"God made him who had no sin to be sin for us, so that in him we might become the righteousness of God" (2 Cor. 5:21 NIV). The parallelism in this passage does not work unless there is a double imputation. Just as God reckoned the sinless Christ as a sinner by imputing to Him our sin, so God reckons us righteous in Christ because the sinlessness of the Lord Jesus has been imputed to us. Jesus was not punished because He actually possessed sin in Himself, just as we are not justified because we actually possess righteousness in ourselves. Rather, both things happen by imputation. Imputation means instead of holding $500 in your hand, someone else wires it to your account. The money is not actually in your physical possession, but it is legally and truthfully considered to be yours. This is what imputation is all about, God counting to us a perfect life of obedience richer than we've ever lived. Thus He grants us a perfect righteousness we have no chance to ever achieve.

57. Q. HOW DOES "THE RESURRECTION OF THE BODY" COMFORT YOU?

A. Not only my soul will be taken immediately after this life to Christ its head, but even my very flesh, raised by the power of Christ, will be reunited with my soul and made like Christ's glorious body.

58. Q. HOW DOES THE ARTICLE CONCERNING "LIFE EVERLASTING" COMFORT YOU?

A. Even as I already now experience in my heart the beginning of eternal joy, so after this life I will have perfect blessedness such as no eye has seen, no ear has heard, no human heart has ever imagined: a blessedness in which to praise God eternally.

Better than the Day Before

*B*efore looking at Lord's Day 22, I want to highlight one small phrase I passed over in Lord's Day 21. Even though the Heidelberg Catechism is most widely used in Reformed churches, its popularity stretches far beyond the walls of Calvinism. Heidelberg is thoroughly Reformed, but not often in a pronounced way like the Canons of Dort. There are only hints of distinctive Reformed leanings. One of those hints is in Answer 54, where the Catechism describes the church as "a community *chosen* for eternal life." The church is not a collection of folks who were smart enough or good enough to find God. The church is a community of those whom God in His goodness chose before the beginning of time (Eph. 1:4). God was the first one to "move" in the relationship. He sought us before we sought Him (John 15:16).

This doctrine of God's free choice or election is not a Reformed invention but the consistent witness of Scripture. The Father gave some to Christ that they might be saved (John 6:37). The Good Shepherd calls His own by name (John 10:3). God appointed some to eternal life (Acts 13:48). He chose us before we had done anything good or bad in order that His purpose might stand and His mercy might be manifest (Rom. 9:10–16). We were called out of the world and into the church not because of works but because of God's purpose and grace given us "in Christ Jesus before the ages began" (2 Tim. 1:9). God chose us not because we were holy but so that we might be holy and blameless in His sight (Eph. 1:4). At the end of the day, the ultimate reason why you believe, while others do not, is not your good choice but because God chose you for eternal life in Christ.

Lord's Day 22 covers the last two phrases of the Apostles' Creed—

"I believe . . . in the resurrection of the body and the life everlasting." Both phrases are for our comfort. When we die we will be away from the body and at home with the Lord (2 Cor. 5:8). This is the intermediate state where we experience the joy of fellowship with Christ even in our disembodied existence. But this is not our final hope. Ultimately we are waiting for the resurrection of our bodies. We will get our material self back. The early African churches used to say, "I believe in the resurrection of *this* flesh," underlining the continuity between our bodily existence in this life and the next. The perishable body will put on the imperishable and the mortal immortality (1 Cor. 15:53). You will still be you in heaven, but you will have a new, better, eternal, flesh-as-it-was-meant-to-be, free from handicap or injury.

It's hard to grasp the goodness and delight of life everlasting, because "no eye has seen, nor ear heard, nor the heart of man imagined" the blessedness that will be ours in the age to come (1 Cor. 2:9). But we must trust that God will not disappoint. Everlasting life is an article of faith ("I believe . . ."). We must believe with longing and hope all that the Bible teaches about our final state. We are meant to think of the end of the story more than we do.

Think about the description of heaven on earth in books like Isaiah and Revelation or in Jesus' parables or in Paul's epistles. It is staggering. Life everlasting means reward, inheritance, blessing, rule, feasting, security, no pain, no mourning, no disappointment, no struggle, no fear. It means a lush garden, a beautiful city, a lasting foundation, a street of gold, a sea of crystal, and a wall of precious stones. It means a wedding celebration, a tree of life, living water, manna from heaven, unending light, and unceasing worship before Him who sits on the throne and unto the Lamb.

The blessedness of eternal life is like savoring your favorite food, drinking your favorite drink, laughing with your favorite friends; it's like seeing your wife on your wedding day sparkling in her overpriced dress and grinning from ear to ear; it's like holding a newborn baby or watching your grandkids play; it's like standing on a dune overlooking Lake Michigan on one side and seeing a sea of green treetops on the other; it's like the peaceful majesty of corn blowing in the breeze in July, or watching an afternoon storm roll over the front range; it's like being awed by a visit to the

Great Wall of China or the skyline in New York City or the York Minster Cathedral in northern England. And it's like that rare moment when you know in your bones that God is with you and you know you really love Him and you want to sing and shout and tell everyone how you feel. It's like all these moments—except the moments never stop and never wane.

Life everlasting is like all of this power, beauty, delight, truth, and sweetness rolled into one experience, then multiplied by ten, then by a hundred, then by ten million. Eternal life in God's presence will be such a weight of glory that we will feel as if we never knew happiness before and all our troubles will be in a moment forgotten as so puny and so trivial and to be utterly inconsequential compared to all this joy.

And this experience of delight and glory will go on forever. On earth, all our joy is fleeting. Food tastes good and is gone. Sex is enjoyable, then it's over. Kids are precious, but they drive you nuts. On earth there is anticipation of pleasure, a moment or season of delight, and then it passes. Joy is always mingled with pain. Delight is always interrupted by suffering. But not in heaven. There, the glory and delight and love are always growing, always swelling, and always increasing as we learn more and see more of God. Every Tuesday is better than Monday. Every Wednesday is better than Tuesday. Every Thursday is better than Wednesday. Nonstop, continuous, everlasting glory. Your best life later (to steal Francis Chan's phrase).

That's the hope. That's the aim. That's the blessedness of praising God and delighting in Him forever and ever.

59. Q. WHAT GOOD DOES IT DO YOU, HOWEVER, TO BELIEVE ALL THIS?

A. In Christ I am right with God and heir to life everlasting.

60. Q. HOW ARE YOU RIGHT WITH GOD?

A. Only by true faith in Jesus Christ. Even though my conscience accuses me of having grievously sinned against all God's commandments and of never having kept any of them, and even though I am still inclined toward all evil, nevertheless, without my deserving it at all, out of sheer grace, God grants and credits to me the perfect satisfaction, righteousness, and holiness of Christ, as if I had never sinned nor been a sinner, as if I had been as perfectly obedient as Christ was obedient for me. All I need to do is to accept this gift of God with a believing heart.

61. Q. WHY DO YOU SAY THAT BY FAITH ALONE YOU ARE RIGHT WITH GOD?

A. It is not because of any value my faith has that God is pleased with me. Only Christ's satisfaction, righteousness, and holiness make me right with God. And I can receive this righteousness and make it mine in no other way than by faith alone.

The Granddaddy
of Them All

From Lord's Days 7 through 22, we've been looking at what we need to believe as Christians. Phrase by phrase, we've worked our way through the Apostles' Creed. After those fourteen "weeks" of doctrinal explanation, Question 59 presents a fair but startling question: "So what?" Okay, so we get the Apostles' Creed, unpack it all, and commit it to memory. Whoop-de-do. What good is it to believe all this?

The answer: In believing all this we are united to Christ, and being united to Christ we are right with God and heirs to life everlasting.

This brings us to the doctrine on which the whole church stands or falls—the granddaddy of them all—the doctrine of *justification*. Without using the word, Lord's Day 23 is all about justification, and whenever the sixteenth-century Reformers talked about justification, they did so very carefully. With new visions and new perspectives on justification buzzing around the church today, it's crucial that we understand the historic Protestant (and I would say biblical!) explanation of justification.

There are five key concepts in the Reformation understanding of justification that find echo in the Catechism.

First, the Christian is *simul iustus et peccator*. This is Martin Luther's famous Latin phrase, which means "at the same time, justified and a sinner." The Catechism powerfully reminds us that even though we are right with God, we still violate His commands, feel the sting of conscience, and battle against indwelling sin. On this side of heaven, we will always be sinning saints, righteous wretches, and on occasion even justified jerks. God does not acquit us of our guilt based on our works but because we trust "him who justifies the ungodly" (Rom. 4:5).

Second, our right standing with God is based on an alien righteousness. "Alien" doesn't refer to an E.T. spirituality. It means we are justified because of a righteousness that is not our own. I am not right with God because of my righteousness, but because "the perfect satisfaction, righteousness, and holiness of Christ" has been credited to me. "Nothing in my hands I bring, simply to thy cross I cling; naked, come to thee for dress; helpless, look to thee for grace; foul, I to the Fountain fly; wash me, Savior, or I die," wrote August Toplady in the old hymn. We contribute nothing to our salvation. The name by which every Christian must be called is "The Lord is our righteousness" (Jer. 23:6).

On a related note, the doctrine of alien righteousness can help ward off all the silly nonsense on our TVs and in our bookstores about finding the god within us. There is much rubbish out there about your inner self or your divine self or your spiritual self and all the powers at your disposal if only you channel it from deep within you. Chesterton said it best: "Of all horrible religions the most horrible is the worship of the god within you. . . . Let Jones worship the sun or moon, anything rather than the Inner Light; let Jones worship cats or crocodiles, if he can find any in his street, but not the god within. Christianity came into the world firstly in order to assert with violence that a man had not only to look inwards, but to look outwards, to behold with astonishment and enthusiasm a divine company and a divine captain. The only fun of being a Christian was that a man was not left alone with the Inner Light, but definitely recognized an outer light, fair as the sun, clear as the moon, terrible as an army with banners."[27] If you can ignore the occasional anti-Calvinist remarks, Chesterton really is a fabulous read.

Third, the righteousness of Christ is ours by imputation, not by impartation. That is to say, we are not *made* holy, or *infused* with goodness as if we possessed it in ourselves, but rather Christ's righteousness is *credited* to our account (see chap. 21).

Fourth, we are justified by faith *alone*. The Catholic Church acknowledged that the Christian was saved by faith; it was the alone part they would not allow. In fact, the Council of Trent from the sixteenth-century Catholic Counter-Reformation declared anathema those who believe in either justification by imputation or justification by faith alone. But evangelical faith has always held that "all I need to do is accept the gift of God with a believing heart." True, justifying faith must show itself in good works. That's what James 2 is all about. But these works serve as corroborating evidence, not as the ground of our justification. We are justified by faith without deeds of the law (Rom. 3:28; Titus 3:5). The gospel is "believe in the Lord Jesus, and you will be saved" (Acts 16:31), not "believe in the Lord Jesus Christ and cooperate with transforming grace and you shall be saved." There is nothing we contribute to our salvation but our sin, no merit we bring but Christ's, and nothing necessary for justification except for faith alone.

Finally, with all this talk about the necessity of faith, the Catechism explains that faith is only an *instrumental* cause in our salvation. In other words, faith is not what God finds acceptable in us. In fact, strictly speaking, faith itself does not justify. Faith is only the instrument by which we embrace Christ, have communion with Him, and share in all His benefits. It is the *object* of our faith that matters. If you venture out onto a frozen pond, it isn't your faith that keeps you from crashing into the water. True, it takes faith to step onto the pond, but it's the object of your faith, the twelve inches of ice, that keeps you safe. Believe in Christ with all your heart, but don't put your faith in your faith. Your experience of trusting Christ will ebb and flow. So be sure to rest in Jesus Christ and not your faith in Him. He alone is the one who died for our sakes and was raised for our justification. Believe this, and you too will be saved.

$\mathcal{L}$ord's Day 24

62. Q. WHY CAN'T THE GOOD WE DO MAKE US RIGHT WITH
GOD, OR AT LEAST HELP MAKE US RIGHT WITH HIM?

A. Because the righteousness which can pass God's scrutiny must be
entirely perfect and must in every way measure up to the divine
law. Even the very best we do in this life is imperfect and stained
with sin.

63. Q. HOW CAN YOU SAY THAT THE GOOD WE DO DOESN'T
EARN ANYTHING WHEN GOD PROMISES TO REWARD IT
IN THIS LIFE AND THE NEXT?

A. This reward is not earned; it is a gift of grace.

64. Q. BUT DOESN'T THIS TEACHING MAKE PEOPLE INDIFFER-
ENT AND WICKED?

A. No. It is impossible for those grafted into Christ by true faith not
to produce fruits of gratitude.

Achieving Low Self-Esteem

*O*ne of the most popular ways of sharing the gospel involves a bridge diagram, where God is on one side of a great chasm and man is on the other. Jesus Christ, then, is the bridge that makes a way for God and man to be reconciled. This is good theology. The only problem is that most people we run into, including perhaps the one you see in front of you as you brush your teeth, do not feel the need to get right with God. We can give people the bridge diagram until they are blue in the face, but if they don't see the chasm between them and God, the availability of a bridge will sound like no news, not good news.

Pelagians are alive and well, even in the church at times. Many no longer believe in original sin. They imagine that God will look kindly on them for their efforts at self-improvement. True, I've never met anyone who thought he was perfect and did everything right in God's eyes. But it is increasingly rare that I meet anyone (except for the evangelical churchgoer and the clinically depressed) who believes in his total moral inability to the extent that he wonders if God might actually be displeased.

I don't want people to be morbidly obsessed with their failings, but the gospel won't be good news if we haven't heard any of the true, bad news. It's hard to be found when you don't know you're lost. Andrew Delbanco, a professor at Columbia University, tells the story of going to an Alcoholics Anonymous meeting for some research he was doing. A young, well-dressed man stood up and gave his personal narrative of addiction. It was full of tales of injustice and betrayal, and mostly full of himself. The young speaker gave the impression of being a proud man who needed to blame others and justify himself. Delbanco says that while this young man was speaking, a black man in his forties, with dread-locks and black shades, leaned over and said, "I used to feel that way too, before I achieved low self-esteem."[28] Good theology that. Pride, Delbanco notes, is always the enemy of hope.

You and I are worse than we think and we can do less to please God than we ever feared on our most dismal day. If you've never felt the chasm between you and God, consider the following:

- God is bigger than we think—holier, more excellent, than we realize.
- We are horribly ungrateful. God gives us life, breath, food, and shelter, and most people "thank" Him by either ignoring Him or wondering if He really exists.
- Our sin consists not just in doing bad things but in making good things the ultimate priority. If we are honest, God is not our first priority on most days.
- If you break even one law, you are still a lawbreaker (James 2:11). If you get pulled over for speeding, the cop won't let you go just because you're up-to-date on your alimony payments.
- "The heart is deceitful above all things, and desperately sick" (Jer. 17:9). We are all proud creatures—proud of being smart, proud of being open-minded, proud of not being so terribly proud.
- Sin is not just what we've done wrong but all the good we have left undone (James 4:17).
- The natural man is unaware of his enmity toward God because he has created a false God in His place. The natural man hates God, but does not sense this hostility because he disbelieves in so much of what he hates.
- Jesus knows we need to get right with God. "Whoever believes in him is not condemned, but whoever does not believe is condemned already" (John 3:18).

So what are we to do with all this unworthiness? Other religions say medi-tate toward enlightenment, or pray so many times a day, or overcome your cravings. The answer Christianity gives is wholly different and somewhat shocking. We do nothing with all our unworthiness. We do nothing to undo our bad doings because we have nothing to contribute but more sin (Isa. 64:6). The reward of eternal life is not a wage we earn but a gift we receive.

Undeserved mercy is the good news and scandal of Christianity. I was talking with a Muslim friend not too long ago, and although we could agree somewhat on God's character and somewhat on human depravity, we did not see mercy the same way. To my friend, Allah is merciful, but there is still a weighing of the balances at the end of the age, still a need for our good deeds to make up for our bad. When I explained the idea of sovereign, free, alien grace at the heart of the Bible, he had one main objection: Doesn't this teaching about salvation by grace alone make people indifferent and wicked? I mean, why do good deeds and deny yourself if such works can do nothing to merit divine favor anyway?

There are three answers to that question: faith, fruit, and gratitude. First, true faith works. It would have been easy for Abraham to say he trusted God when the Lord told him to kill his son. But it wouldn't have been true faith unless Abraham raised the knife in the air and was ready to plunge it into Isaac. Saving faith is not mere intellectual assent but a firm trust, played out in real life, that God's promises are true and His promises do not fail.

Second, a good tree bears good fruit. If we have truly been regenerated by the Spirit of God and given new spiritual life, we will show the effects. If we live habitually as selfish, God-ignoring, sin-cherishing people, then we haven't really been changed, and we haven't really experienced grace.

Finally, grace does not lead to license because grace leads to gratitude. If I was called up to play for the Chicago White Sox, with my inability to hit a ball off a tee, my response would not be laziness but hard work. I would be so stunned by the absurd unworthiness of the call that in addition to being very thankful, I would be motivated not to disappoint. Gratitude brings the good works.

65. Q. IT IS BY FAITH ALONE THAT WE SHARE IN CHRIST AND ALL HIS BLESSINGS: WHERE THEN DOES THAT FAITH COME FROM?

A. The Holy Spirit produces it in our hearts by the preaching of the holy gospel, and confirms it through our use of the holy sacraments.

66. Q. WHAT ARE SACRAMENTS?

A. Sacraments are holy signs and seals for us to see. They were instituted by God so that by our use of them He might make us understand more clearly the promise of the gospel, and might put His seal on that promise. And this is God's gospel promise: to forgive our sins and give us eternal life by grace alone because of Christ's one sacrifice finished on the cross.

67. Q. ARE BOTH THE WORD AND THE SACRAMENTS THEN INTENDED TO FOCUS OUR FAITH ON THE SACRIFICE OF JESUS CHRIST ON THE CROSS AS THE ONLY GROUND OF OUR SALVATION?

A. Right! In the gospel the Holy Spirit teaches us and through the holy sacraments He assures us that our entire salvation rests on Christ's one sacrifice for us on the cross.

68. Q. HOW MANY SACRAMENTS DID CHRIST INSTITUTE IN THE NEW TESTAMENT?

A. Two: baptism and the Lord's Supper.

Visible Signs of
Invisible Grace

*C*onflicts within the church are nothing new. Each age of the church's history had its issues. First it was the Jew-Gentile question. Then came the doctrine of the Trinity in the fourth century at Nicea. Shortly after that, the church wrestled with Pelagianism and the human inability to live a righteous life. Then the person of Christ got hammered out at Chalcedon in the middle of the fifth century (and the debate began long before that). During the Reformation, justification was the key issue. In the nineteenth century eschatology, loomed large. In the twentieth century, the authority of Scripture was challenged. Today the issues involve the uniqueness of Christ in a pluralistic world and the unchanging standards of biblical sexuality. There will always be something.

In the sixteenth century, the doctrine of the sacraments was another one of those hot issues. I'd wager a guess that most of us don't think a lot about the sacraments (or ordinances, as they're sometimes called). Sure, there are the high church folks who are always talking about "their baptism" and Eucharistic this and that. But for nondenominational evangelical Joe, the sacraments are *terra nova*. Many evangelicals see more movie clips in church during the year than they see sacraments. But next to the doctrine of justification by faith alone, the Reformers wrote about the sacraments more than any other issue. And while they also fought among themselves over the sacraments, the Reformers did agree on a number of key points. We see four of them in this Lord's Day.

First, we are not saved by the sacraments but by faith alone. In the medieval church, many Christians had a superstitious view of the sacraments. This is why the Reformers objected to the Latin phrase *ex opere operato* ("from the work having been worked"). The Catholic Church taught the sacraments worked objectively based on the dispensing of the sacraments themselves. To the extent that *ex opere operato* insists on the validity of the sacraments despite the moral unworthiness of the one administering it, we are on solid ground. But from the Catholic understanding of *ex opere operato*, many churchgoers expected the sacraments to impart grace by some kind of magic, irrespective of their faith. But the Bible is clear: We are not saved just by virtue of having been baptized or having received Communion; we must have faith. The sacraments are means of grace only insofar as we receive by faith the gospel truths promised in the elements.

Second, the Reformers agreed, against the Roman Catholic Church, that the number of sacraments instituted by Christ was only two: baptism and the Lord's Supper (Q/A 68). The Catholic Church has five other sacraments, none of which are explicitly instituted by Christ and attached to a promise. *Confirmation*—anointing for salvation in the triune name— is nowhere commanded in Scripture. *Holy Orders*, or the laying on of hands, has biblical precedence but the ordination scheme in the Catholic Church is an elaborate postbiblical design. *Penance* hints at our need to be reminded of the forgiveness of sins, but remembering our baptism does the same thing. *Extreme Unction*, or last rites, or anointing the sick with holy oil, has its roots in James 5, but the sign is not commanded by the Lord. *Marriage* as a sacrament is based on a mistranslation of Ephesians 5:32 in the Latin Vulgate. By contrast, baptism is required of every disciple as symbolic of the forgiveness of sins (Matt. 28:19; Acts 2:38) and the Lord's Supper was clearly instituted by Christ (1 Cor. 11:23ff) and celebrated regularly, if not weekly (Acts 2:42).

Third, the Reformers agreed that the sacraments could in no way add to or repeat Christ's one sacrifice on the cross. The sacraments do not "accomplish" anything, because Christ's work is already finished. As we'll see in Lord's Day 30, Catholics saw the Mass as a reenactment of Jesus' death, but this expects too much from signs and seals. The Catechism is right: "our entire salvation rests on Christ's one sacrifice for us on the cross."

Fourth, as was just mentioned, the sacraments are signs and seals. We come to faith through hearing the gospel, not through the water of baptism, nor from taking the bread and wine. The sacraments do not create faith; rather, they confirm it, make us understand the gospel promises more clearly, and assure us of our salvation. As we'll see in the coming Lord's Days, the sacraments are meant to nourish our faith, strengthen us, prop us up, and assure us of God's favor. They are holy signs symbolizing the spiritual realities of the gospel, and seals reminding us of God's sure promises.

The whole point in this sign and seal business is that we can *see* the sacraments. Hence, Augustine's oft-quoted definition that the sacraments are visible means of an invisible grace. We often forget amidst the calls for sensory worship and appeals to visual learning styles that God has already given us His own self-appointed means of using our senses in worship. He's given us the sacraments that we might see, smell, taste, and touch the same promises of the gospel we hear proclaimed in the preaching of the Word.

69. Q. HOW DOES BAPTISM REMIND YOU AND ASSURE YOU THAT CHRIST'S ONE SACRIFICE ON THE CROSS IS FOR YOU PERSONALLY?

A. In this way: Christ instituted this outward washing and with it gave the promise that, as surely as water washes away the dirt from the body, so certainly His blood and His Spirit wash away my soul's impurity, in other words, all my sins.

70. Q. WHAT DOES IT MEAN TO BE WASHED WITH CHRIST'S BLOOD AND SPIRIT?

A. To be washed with Christ's blood means that God, by grace, has forgiven my sins because of Christ's blood poured out for me in His sacrifice on the cross. To be washed with Christ's Spirit means that the Holy Spirit has renewed me and set me apart to be a member of Christ so that more and more I become dead to sin and increasingly live a holy and blameless life.

71. Q. WHERE DOES CHRIST PROMISE THAT WE ARE WASHED WITH HIS BLOOD AND SPIRIT AS SURELY AS WE ARE WASHED WITH THE WATER OF BAPTISM?

A. In the institution of baptism where He says: "Therefore go and make disciples of all nations, baptizing them in the name of the Father and of the Son and of the Holy Spirit." "Whoever believes and is baptized will be saved, but whoever does not believe will be condemned." This promise is repeated when Scripture calls baptism the washing of rebirth and the washing away of sins.

Clean! Clean!

The Great Commission in Matthew 28, as I've told my congregation many times, has one imperative verb and three supporting participles. The main verb is not "go," though it looks like it in our English translations. The main verb is the command "make disciples." The three participles explain how the command is fulfilled. We make disciples of all nations by going, baptizing, and teaching them to obey all that Jesus has commanded. We understand the going part of the Great Commission. That's why we have missions week. We get the teaching part too. That's the whole point in going. But many of us don't think a lot about the baptizing part. And yet, Jesus makes it one of the key elements in fulfilling the Great Commission. So it must be crucially important.

Baptism is a central component of the Great Commission because baptism marks us out as a follower of Christ and assures us that by faith we have been forgiven by God. There's a lot that can be said about the meaning of baptism. It signifies our dying and rising with Christ. It signifies our sprinkling with the blood of Christ. It signifies our union with Christ. All of this is true and worth our contemplation. But at the most basic level, the water of baptism reminds us that our sins have been washed away. All our stains have been wiped clean by the sin-scrubbing detergent of God's grace.

We don't think of our baptism enough. Whether you were baptized as an adult or a child or even as an infant, you should think of your baptism often. This may mean remembering the actual event of your baptism or simply remembering that you are baptized and have been sealed with the promise of God's forgiveness. When you trip up and overeat to the point of gluttony, when you lose it with your kids, when you lament that you have such a critical spirit, you should remember your baptism. By faith you are forgiven and have been washed clean. Baptism is that reminder, a symbol of forgiveness we have received (as noted in Question 72 of Lord's Day 27).

We don't have cable, but the other day I was staying at a house that did. On a lazy afternoon I turned on the TV and flipped through the stations about four times, looking in vain for something interesting to watch. I eventually stopped for about sixty seconds on some TV movie. It didn't take long before the scene got racy, one of those times where they don't show anything but it suggested a perverse action. I pretty quickly changed the channel, but only *pretty* quickly. If I'm honest, I stopped at the channel in the first place because I noticed the way the women were dressed. And I lingered for a few more seconds even after I saw that the scene was going nowhere but down into the gutter. The scene was sensual and turning to it was sin.

I felt terrible. I tried to justify myself in my mind. *It was just a few seconds. They didn't show anything. It wasn't like I was downloading porn. It was just cable.* Just cable?! What a lame excuse. The simple fact is there is no excuse for sin, not for your sin, nor for mine. But after the sin I began to think of this Lord's Day: "As surely as water washes away the dirt from the body, so certainly His blood and His Spirit wash away my soul's impurity."

I was baptized as a little baby decades ago, but the promise of God's grace is no less real to me. I got wet that day (even if my Baptist friends don't think I got wet enough!). I was washed. My sins were not magically wiped away by the water. But the promise of God's cleansing signed to me that day is mine through faith. When I confess my sins, God is always faithful to forgive (1 John 1:7–9). Just as surely as the water was sprinkled over my little head (or washed over your whole body as the case may be), so surely have I been made clean by the blood of Christ. That black mark of sixty seconds on cable television (and believe me, that's not the worst thing I've ever done!) has been washed away.

When I was younger I used to actually exert myself physically. I climbed a lot of trees, played a lot of sports, and got dirty like boys are supposed to. I never minded a little dirt, but I liked to get clean at the end of the day. That's why I shower at night instead of in the morning. I don't need to get clean before I start the day. I need to get clean at the end of the day. Every day, I need to get spiritually clean too. So every day I have reason to remember my baptism. By the end of each day, there is sinful crud and junk clinging to my body. I need to visit the cross. I need to be washed. Praise God for the blood that saves instead of stains. Praise God I have been baptized in the name of the Father and of the Son and of the Holy Spirit.

72. Q. DOES THIS OUTWARD WASHING WITH WATER ITSELF WASH AWAY SINS?

A. No, only Jesus Christ's blood and the Holy Spirit cleanse us from all sins.

73. Q. WHY THEN DOES THE HOLY SPIRIT CALL BAPTISM THE WASHING OF REBIRTH AND THE WASHING AWAY OF SINS?

A. God has good reason for these words. He wants to teach us that the blood and Spirit of Christ wash away our sins just as water washes away dirt from our bodies. But more important, He wants to assure us, by this divine pledge and sign, that the washing away of our sins spiritually is as real as physical washing with water.

74. Q. SHOULD INFANTS, TOO, BE BAPTIZED?

A. Yes. Infants as well as adults are in God's covenant and are His people. They, no less than adults, are promised the forgiveness of sin through Christ's blood and the Holy Spirit who produces faith. Therefore, by baptism, the mark of the covenant, infants should be received into the Christian church and should be distinguished from the children of unbelievers. This was done in the Old Testament by circumcision, which was replaced in the New Testament by baptism.

Vivacious Baby-Baptizing

*O*f all the things I've been called on blogs and in reviews, my favorite came from a Baptist brother who said I might be "the most vivacious baby-baptizer in the world." I'm not sure about vivacious, but I am a proud baby-baptizer. My assumption (and hope) is that many people reading this book do not practice infant baptism. I have many friends, colleagues, and heroes in the faith who do not agree with me (and others of my friends, colleagues, and heroes) on the issue of baptism. So I undertake my brief defense of infant baptism in this chapter in the spirit of respect and appreciation for my credobaptist brothers and sisters.

One of the best things I get to do as a pastor is to administer the sacrament of infant baptism to the covenant children in my congregation. Before each baptism, I take a few minutes to explain why we practice infant baptism in our church. My explanation usually goes something like this:

"It is our great privilege this morning to administer the sacrament of baptism to one of our little infants. We do not believe that there is anything magical about the water we apply to the child. The water does not wash away original sin or save the child. We do not presume that this child is regenerate, nor do we believe that every child who gets baptized will automatically go to heaven. We baptize infants not out of superstition or tradition or because we like cute babies. We baptize infants because they are covenant children and should receive the sign of the covenant.

"In Genesis 15 God made a covenant with Abraham. This covenant was sealed with the sign of circumcision in Genesis 17. God promised to bless Abraham. For Abraham this meant two things in particular, offspring and land. But at the heart of the covenant was God's promise that He would be a God to Abraham and his children (Gen. 17:7–8).

"Circumcision was not just a physical thing, marking out ethnic Jews. Circumcision was full of spiritual meaning. The circumcision of the flesh was always meant to correspond with circumcision of the heart (Rom. 2:25–29). It pointed to humility, new birth, and a new way of life (Lev. 26:40–42; Deut. 10:16; 30:6; Jer. 4:4; 6:10; 9:25). In short, circumcision was a sign of justification. Paul says in Romans 4:11 that Abraham 'received the sign of circumcision as a seal of the righteousness that he had by faith while he was still uncircumcised.' God's own interpretation of circumcision is that it was much more than just a physical sign for national Israel.

"Remarkably, though, this deeply spiritual sign was given to Ishmael as well as Isaac, even though only Isaac was the continuation of the promised line. The spiritual sign was not just for those who already embraced the spiritual reality. It was to be administered to Abraham and his sons. Circumcision was not a simple equation. It didn't automatically mean the recipient of the sign was in possession of the thing signified. Circumcision, like baptism, also pointed to belonging, discipleship, covenant obligations, and allowed for future faith that would take hold of the realities symbolized. Just as there were some in Paul's day who were circumcised but not really circumcised (Rom. 2:25–29), some children of Abraham who were not truly children of Abraham (Rom. 9:6–8), so in our day there are some who are baptized who are not truly baptized. Children should be marked as belonging to the covenant, but unless they exercise saving faith, they will not grab hold of the covenant blessings.

"Children today are baptized based on this same covenant with Abraham. Paul makes clear in Galatians 3 what Peter strongly suggests in Acts 2, namely, that the Abrahamic covenant has not been annulled. It is still operational. In fact, we see the basic promise of the Abrahamic covenant running throughout the whole Bible, right up to the new heaven and new earth in Revelation 21.

"Because sons were part of the Abrahamic covenant in the Old Testament and were circumcised, we see no reason why children should be excluded in the New Testament sign of baptism. Admittedly, there is no text that says 'Hear ye, hear ye, baptism replaces circumcision.' But we know from Colossians 2:11–12 that baptism and circumcision carried the same spiritual import. The transition from one to the other was probably organic. As the Jews practiced proselyte baptism, that sign came to be seen as marking inclusion in the covenant people. For a while circumcision existed along with baptism, but as the early church became more Gentile, many of the Jewish rites were rendered unnecessary, and sometimes even detrimental to the faith. Thus, baptism eclipsed circumcision as the sign of renewal, rebirth, and covenant membership."

Then I tell the congregation of several other arguments that support a paedobaptist reading of the New Testament.

"One, the burden of proof rests on those who would deny children a sign they had received for thousands of years. If children were suddenly outside the covenant, and were disallowed from receiving any 'sacramental' sign, surely such a massive change, and the controversy that would have ensued, would have been recorded in the New Testament. Moreover, it would be strange for children to be excluded from the covenant, when everything else moves in the direction of more inclusion from the old covenant to the new.

"Two, the existence of household baptisms is evidence that God still deals with households as a unit and welcomes whole families into the church to come under the lordship of Christ together [Acts 16:13–15, 32–34; 1 Cor. 1:16; cf. Josh. 24:15].

"Three, children are told to obey their parents *in the Lord* (Eph. 6:1). Children in the church are not treated as little pagans to be evangelized, but members of the covenant who owe their allegiance to Christ.

"Four, Christ welcomed little children to Himself and blessed them (Mark 10:13–16). The Israelites would not have understood this as a casual sort of 'God bless and good luck.' They would have thought of the blessing promised to Abraham (Gen. 12) and the blessings given through Moses (Lev. 26; Deut. 28). These were blessings belonging to the covenant that Jesus pronounced on the children.

"Five, within two centuries we have clear evidence that the church was practicing infant baptism.[29] If this had been a change to long-standing tradition, we would have some record of the church arguing over this new practice. It wasn't until the sixteenth century that Christians began to question this practice.

"So we come to administer the sacrament of baptism to this child today with the weight of church history to encourage us and the example of redemptive history to confirm our practice. We baptize in obedience to Christ's command. The sacrament we are about to administer is a sign of inclusion in the covenant community as circumcision was, and the water we are about to sprinkle is a sign of cleansing from sin as the sprinkled blood of bulls and goats in the Old Testament was. We pray that this little one will take advantage of all his covenant privileges, acknowledge his Lord all the days of his life, and by faith make these promises his own."

75. Q. HOW DOES THE LORD'S SUPPER REMIND YOU AND ASSURE YOU THAT YOU SHARE IN CHRIST'S ONE SACRIFICE ON THE CROSS AND IN ALL HIS GIFTS?

A. In this way: Christ has commanded me and all believers to eat this broken bread and to drink this cup. With this command He gave this promise: First, as surely as I see with my eyes the bread of the Lord broken for me and the cup given to me, so surely His body was offered and broken for me and His blood poured out for me on the cross. Second, as surely as I receive from the hand of the one who serves, and taste with my mouth the bread and cup of the Lord, given me as sure signs of Christ's body and blood, so surely He nourishes and refreshes my soul for eternal life with His crucified body and poured-out blood.

76. Q. WHAT DOES IT MEAN TO EAT THE CRUCIFIED BODY OF CHRIST AND TO DRINK HIS POURED-OUT BLOOD?

A. It means to accept with a believing heart the entire suffering and death of Christ and by believing to receive forgiveness of sins and eternal life. But it means more. Through the Holy Spirit, who lives both in Christ and in us, we are united more and more to Christ's blessed body. And so, although He is in heaven and we are on earth, we are flesh of His flesh and bone of His bone. And we forever live on and are governed by one Spirit, as members of our body are by one soul.

77. Q. WHERE DOES CHRIST PROMISE TO NOURISH AND REFRESH BELIEVERS WITH HIS BODY AND BLOOD AS SURELY AS THEY EAT THIS BROKEN BREAD AND DRINK THIS CUP?

A. [The Catechism quotes from 1 Corinthians 11:23–26 and 1 Corinthians 10:16–17.]

"As Surely"

I am not a prolific crier. I can think of only three or four times I've been visibly choked up in front of my congregation. One of those times came while reading this Lord's Day in preparation for Communion. After the service, I had others tell me they started to cry too. I love good music in church and rejoice to see God's people emotionally engaged in worship. But if our emotion is to be truth driven and not just melody driven, we ought to have profound experiences with responsive readings, creeds, and confessions too. Every time we read the Nicene Creed, I want to raise my hands in the air (and sometimes do). And whenever I read through this Lord's Day before Communion, it almost makes me want to cry.

What good news God proclaims to us at the Table—what a visible sign of God's grace we enjoy! As surely as I know, without any doubt or hesitation, that I am holding bread and sipping juice, so surely can I know, with complete confidence, God loves me in Christ.

I fear that in most churches the Lord's Supper is either celebrated so infrequently as to be forgotten or celebrated with such thoughtless monotony that churchgoers endure it rather than enjoy it. But the Lord's Supper is meant to nourish and strengthen our weak faith. Have you ever come to church feeling dirty for the way you stared at the young woman at the Gap? Have you ever sat through an entire sermon thinking about how you blew up at your kids that morning or how prayerless you've been for the past month? Have you ever come to the end of a church service only to think, *I'm so distracted. I keep thinking about football?* Or, *I keep thinking about getting ready for the company we're having over. I can't even sit through church right?* Have you ever wondered if God can really be for you when you are oblivious to Him so much of the time?? If so, you need this gospel Table.

The Lord knows our faith is weak. That's why He's given us sacraments to see, taste, and touch. As surely as you can see the bread and cup, so surely does God love you through Christ. As surely as you chew the food and drain the drink, so surely has Christ died for you. Here at the Table, the faith becomes sight. The simple bread and cup give assurance that Christ came for you, Christ died for you, Christ is coming again for you. Whenever we eat the bread and drink from the cup, we not only reproclaim the Lord's death until He comes again (1 Cor. 11:26), we reconvince ourselves of God's provision on the cross.

Too many churches overlook God's preferred visual aids—the sacraments—and jump right to video, drama, and props to get people's attention. We are making a big mistake when we think these "signs and seals" will be anywhere as effective as the ones instituted by Christ Himself. Pastors who don't explain the sacraments and very rarely administer them are robbing their people of tremendous encouragement in their Christian walk. We can hear the gospel every Sunday, and eat it too.

Of course, this eating and drinking must be undertaken in faith. The elements themselves do not save us. But when we eat and drink them in faith, we can be assured that we receive forgiveness of sins and eternal life. More than that, we get a picture of our union with Christ. As we eat His flesh and drink His blood, we literally have communion with Him, not by dragging Christ down from heaven but by experiencing His presence through His Spirit. Shame on parishioners for coming to the Lord's Supper with nothing but drudgery and low expectations. And shame on pastors for not instructing their people in the gospel joy available to us in Communion.

If you shed a tear at the Table, let it not be out of boredom but out of gratitude and sheer delight.

Lord's Day 29

78. Q. ARE THE BREAD AND WINE CHANGED INTO THE REAL BODY AND BLOOD OF CHRIST?

A. No. Just as the water of baptism is not changed into Christ's blood and does not itself wash away sins but is simply God's sign and assurance, so too the bread of the Lord's Supper is not changed into the actual body of Christ even though it is called the body of Christ in keeping with the nature and language of sacraments.

79. Q. WHY THEN DOES CHRIST CALL THE BREAD HIS BODY AND THE CUP HIS BLOOD, OR THE NEW COVENANT IN HIS BLOOD? (PAUL USES THE WORDS, A PARTICIPATION IN CHRIST'S BODY AND BLOOD.)

A. Christ has good reason for these words. He wants to teach us that as bread and wine nourish our temporal life, so too His crucified body and poured-out blood truly nourish our souls for eternal life. But more important, He wants to assure us, by this visible sign and pledge, that we, through the Holy Spirit's work, share in His true body and blood as surely as our mouths receive these holy signs in His remembrance, and that all of His suffering and obedience are as definitely ours as if we personally had suffered and paid for our sins.

A Real Presence?

$\mathcal{N}$ext to justification, there was no issue more fiercely debated during the Reformation than the doctrine of the Lord's Supper. Although the Reformers did not always agree among themselves as to the meaning of the sacrament, they were unified in their opposition to the Roman Catholic view. Catholics believe in what's called transubstantiation. That is, they believe the bread and the wine become the actual body and blood of Christ. Using categories from Aristotle, Catholics teach that the substance of the elements is changed while the accidents remain the same. This is how the elements can be transubstantiated, but still retain the outer appearance of bread and wine.

According to Catholic teaching, when Jesus held up the bread in the upper room and said, "This is my body," He meant "This loaf of bread is my actual, real physical body." The Reformers, alluding to the Latin phrase *hoc est corpus meum* ("this is my body"), derided the Catholic view as hocus pocus. They argued instead that Jesus was employing a figure of speech. Just as "I am the good Shepherd" did not mean Jesus tended little animals that go baa-baa, and "I am the gate" did not mean Jesus swung on hinges, and "Whoever believes in me . . . out of his heart will flow rivers of living water" did not mean that the disciples would rupture a valve with H_2O, so "This is my body" did not mean "This loaf is my actual flesh and bone" (cf. 1 Cor. 10:4).

Luther and his followers rejected transubstantiation, but they did not completely reject a real physical presence of Christ. Lutherans hold to the doctrine of consubstantiation. They believe the bread is real bread and the wine is real wine, but the physical presence of Christ is there also, "in, with, and under" the elements.

A third view of the Lord's Supper, called the memorial view, is often attributed to Ulrich Zwingli, though it's not clear this captures the fullness of his thought. In this view, Communion is simply a feast of remembrance. There is nothing mystical about it, no real presence to fuss about. The bread and wine remain plain old bread and wine. They serve as a reminder of Christ's sacrifice, a memorial to His death for our sins.

The fourth view is associated with John Calvin. Not surprisingly it is the view represented in the Catechism. Calvin believed the Supper was a feast of remembrance. But he believed it was a feast of communion too. He believed in a real presence, a real spiritual presence whereby we feast on Christ by faith and experience His presence through the ministry of the Holy Spirit. By faith, then, we "share in His true body and blood" (Answer 79).

Clearly, the Lord's Supper is a memorial. We remember Christ's Last Supper (1 Cor. 11:23–25). We remember His sacrifice and proclaim His death (1 Cor. 11:26). But the Lord's Supper is also a communion. First Corinthians 10:16 says, "The cup of blessing that we bless, is it not a participation [*koinonia*] in the blood of Christ? The bread that we break, is it not a participation [*koinonia*] in the body of Christ?" When we drink the cup and eat the bread, we participate in, have fellowship with, the body and blood of Christ. We are joined to Him and experience a deep, spiritual *koinonia* with Him. Christ is truly present with us at the Table.

But even this does not exhaust the meaning of the Lord's Supper. We proclaim the Lord's death until He comes (1 Cor. 11:26). We participate in the benefits of Christ's death. We gain spiritual nourishment (John 6:53–57). And we give a sign of our unity as believers (1 Cor. 10:17). In all of this the Lord's Supper acts as a family table where we can enjoy fellowship with each other and partake of the rich feast of blessings purchased for us at the cross of Christ.[30]

Lord's Day 30

80. **Q.** HOW DOES THE LORD'S SUPPER DIFFER FROM THE ROMAN CATHOLIC MASS?

A. The Lord's Supper declares to us that our sins have been completely forgiven through the one sacrifice of Jesus Christ which He Himself finished on the cross once for all. It also declares to us that the Holy Spirit grafts us into Christ, who with His very body is now in heaven at the right hand of the Father where He wants us to worship Him. But the Mass teaches that the living and the dead do not have their sins forgiven through the suffering of Christ unless Christ is still offered for them daily by the priests. It also teaches that Christ is bodily present in the form of bread and wine where Christ is therefore to be worshiped. Thus the Mass is basically nothing but a denial of the one sacrifice and suffering of Jesus Christ and a condemnable idolatry.

81. **Q.** WHO ARE TO COME TO THE LORD'S TABLE?

A. Those who are displeased with themselves because of their sins, but who nevertheless trust that their sins are pardoned and that their continuing weakness is covered by the suffering and death of Christ, and who also desire more and more to strengthen their faith and to lead a better life. Hypocrites and those who are unrepentant, however, eat and drink judgment on themselves.

82. **Q.** ARE THOSE TO BE ADMITTED TO THE LORD'S SUPPER WHO SHOW BY WHAT THEY SAY AND DO THAT THEY ARE UNBELIEVING AND UNGODLY?

A. No, that would dishonor God's covenant and bring down God's anger upon the entire congregation. Therefore, according to the instruction of Christ and His apostles, the Christian church is duty-bound to exclude such people, by the official use of the keys of the kingdom, until they reform their lives.

The Lord's Supper
and the Mass:
How Wide the Divide?

I love how pastoral the Catechism is. Those who write off catechisms as dry and dusty, as freeze-dried dogma, have never read this one. Isn't it comforting to know that the Lord's Table is not for those who smile all the time and have great self-esteem, but for those who are "displeased with themselves because of their sins" (Answer 81)? The Supper is for those with "continuing weakness" who, although they are seriously flawed, "desire more and more to strengthen their faith and to lead a better life."

Communion is for the weak, but it is not for the hypocrite. Hypocrites are not those who live worse than they profess—that's all of us. Hypocrites are those who cannot see, or are not honest about the gap between their talk and their walk. The Table is for those who hate their sins, not for those who coddle them or excuse them or make no effort to turn from them. These persons must not be admitted to the Lord's Supper, lest they "dishonor God's covenant" and "bring God's anger upon the entire congregation" (Answer 82). First Corinthians 11 has some frightening verses: "Whoever, therefore, eats the bread or drinks the cup of the Lord in an unworthy manner will be guilty concerning the body and blood of the Lord. Let a person examine himself, then, and so eat of the bread and drink of the cup. For anyone who eats and drinks without discerning the body eats and drinks judgment on himself. That is why many of you are weak and ill, and some have died" (11:27–30).

To partake of the Lord's Supper in an unworthy manner is to show contempt for the Lord's covenant and, hence, to merit God's covenant curses on His covenant people. And if you think this is a difficult word to swallow, now we move to something more controversial.

Heidelberg is famous for being an irenic document. There is no nailing of Lutherans to the wall, or drowning of Anabaptists, and very little anathematizing Catholics in the spirit of "What goes around comes around." But there is this concluding line from Answer 80 where Ursinus and his buddies take the gloves off: "Thus the Mass is basically nothing but a denial of the one sacrifice and suffering of Jesus Christ and a condemnable idolatry." True, as almost every English translation points out, Q/A 80 was not present in the first edition (January 1563) of the Catechism. But the present form was included by the third edition (published later in 1563) and has always been the standard received text. In fact, the first edition was lost until 1864. Ever since then, Q/A 80 has been considered a part of the Catechism as much any other question and answer.

So what are we to make of this harsh language in Answer 80? Well, before assessing the rightness or wrongness of Lord's Day 30, we need some historical background. Unlike Protestant services where the sermon is the focal point, in the Catholic worship service, or Mass, the main event is the Eucharist (what Protestants call the Lord's Supper or Communion). The priest may give a ten-minute homily on a passage of Scripture, but the Eucharistic celebration is what makes Mass a Mass.

At the heart of the Catholic understanding of the Eucharist is a belief in the real "substantial" body and blood of Christ in the bread and the wine. Catholics believe that the elements are transubstantiated, so that when consecrated by the priest, the bread and wine actually become the flesh and blood of Christ. For Catholics, the Lord's Supper is not just a memorial service remembering Christ's death, or even a spiritual presence where we feast on Christ in a mystical, spiritual way. The Eucharist, in the Catholic tradition, is also a sacrifice.

And this is what the authors of the Heidelberg Catechism found so offensive in the Catholic Mass. In fact, the reason the Catechism added Q/A 80 in the third edition was, most likely, in order to respond to the Council of Trent. On September 17, 1562, the twenty-second session of the Council of Trent, the official arm of the Catholic Counter-Reformation, met and issued a statement "on the sacrifice of the Mass." (The first edition of the Heidelberg Catechism was not able to touch on Trent's statement, which is why a revision several months later was necessary.) The Council of Trent pronounced, in no uncertain terms, that the Mass was a re-presenting, not just symbolically but actually, of Christ's atoning death.[31]

To be fair, Catholic theology does not consider the Eucharist a re-sacrifice of Christ. "The sacrifice of Christ and the sacrifice of the Eucharist are *one single sacrifice* . . ." (*Catechism of the Catholic Church*, 1367). Thus, Catholic theologians do not agree with the Heidelberg that the Mass is "nothing but a denial of the one sacrifice and suffering of Jesus Christ." The sacrifice of Christ and the Eucharist are one sacrifice performed in different ways, they would argue. Official Catholic teaching does not argue that Christ's death must be repeated over and over. Rather, it teaches that in the Eucharist the death of Christ is pulled into the present for us to enjoy sacramentally.[32] No Catholic who knows his official theology would claim that the Mass repeats the atoning sacrifice of Christ, because the sacrifice is "ever present" (CCC 1364). So the wording of the Catechism does not reflect the way Catholic theology understands the Mass (resulting in an emendation by the Christian Reformed Church).[33]

But, on a popular level, I wonder how many Catholics attending Mass understand this nuance. Even though the Heidelberg does not describe the Catholic position entirely accurately, it is easy to understand how talk of a propitiatory sacrifice in the Eucharistic looks a lot like repeating Christ's once-and-for-all, never-to-be-repeated sacrifice (Heb. 9:25–26; 10:10–18). At the very least we can object to: (1) the notion that the finished work of Christ (John 19:30) is somehow atemporal and can be pulled into the present, (2) the belief that the Mass is in any way a sacrifice for sins, and (3) the idea that the elements become the actual body and blood of Christ.

More to the point, though I would rather not reignite Protestant-Catholic polemics, I have to say that I still think the Catholic adoration of Christ in the bread and wine is offensive to God. "Condemnable" is not the right word. I believe there are individual Catholics who trust in Jesus Christ alone and are saved by faith apart from works. But the way Catholics celebrate the Eucharist is profoundly mistaken.

Is it idolatrous as the Heidelberg Catechism suggests? The argument that it could be, though not the conclusion that it is, finds confirmation in a surprising place: Catholic apologists.

In their book about coming "home" to Rome, popular Catholic apologist Scott Hahn and his wife, Kimberly, relate their initial experiences with the Mass. Kimberly explains:

"One evening, we had an opportunity to be at a Mass where there was a Eucharistic procession at the end. I had never seen this before. As I watched row after row of grown men and women kneel and bow when the monstrance[34] passed by, I thought, These people believe that this is the Lord, and not just bread and wine. If this is Jesus, that is the only appropriate response. If one should kneel before a king today, how much more before the King of Kings? the Lord of Lords? Is it safe to kneel or not?

"But, I continued to ruminate, what if it's not?" she asks. "If that is not Jesus in the monstrance, then what they are doing is gross idolatry."[35]

Peter Kreeft, another winsome Roman Catholic, says something similar: "If the doctrine of the Real Presence of Christ in the Eucharist were not true, this adoration would be the most momentous idolatry: bowing to bread and worshipping wine! And if it *is* true, then to refuse to adore is equally monstrous."[36] There's no way around this dilemma. If transubstantiation is true, then the Mass is pleasing to God and we ought to bow before the consecrated host. But if "This is My body" is to be taken no more concretely than "I am the gate," and if the doctrine of transubstantiation only works by importing Aristotelian categories, then Protestant fears about the Mass are justified. It is not safe to kneel.

Kreeft thinks it is shocking that I would not bow to the bread and wine in a Mass because he believes Christ is visibly present[37] there. I think it is shocking to bow to the bread and wine because I do not believe Christ is visibly present there. Both sides cannot be right. One side is making a sinful mistake. The Heidelberg Catechism asserts the Catholic view of the Mass is mistaken. I agree. The same person who died on Calvary 2,000 years ago is not sacrificed on the altar for our sins during the Eucharistic celebration. Therefore, following the logic laid out by Catholics themselves, Protestants, who reject Rome's interpretation of John 6, must conclude that parts of the Mass are idolatrous.

Granted, the intention of sincere Catholics is to worship Christ, as He is present in the bread and wine. They do not see themselves as worshiping a wafer. But the wafer is physically no more than a wafer. When Jesus says "this cup . . . is the new covenant" (Luke 22:20), we don't equate an actual cup with the new covenant. So why would we take "this is my body" (Luke 22:19) to mean that the bread has become the actual body of Christ?

There is no Real Presence in the Eucharist as Catholics have understood it since the Fourth Lateran Council (1215). All of this means the Lord's Supper is to be celebrated not on an altar, but around a table (1 Cor. 11:20). The only altar we have is the cross (Heb. 13:10; 7:27; 10:10), and the only ongoing sacrifices are the praises on our lips (13:15) and the obedience of our lives (Rom. 12:1).

83. Q. WHAT ARE THE KEYS OF THE KINGDOM?

A. The preaching of the holy gospel and Christian discipline toward repentance. Both preaching and discipline open the kingdom of heaven to believers and close it to unbelievers.

84. Q. HOW DOES PREACHING THE GOSPEL OPEN AND CLOSE THE KINGDOM OF HEAVEN?

A. According to the command of Christ: The kingdom of heaven is opened by proclaiming and publicly declaring to all believers, each and every one, that, as often as they accept the gospel promise in true faith, God, because of what Christ has done, truly forgives all their sins. The kingdom of heaven is closed, however, by proclaiming and publicly declaring to unbelievers and hypocrites that, as long as they do not repent, the anger of God and eternal condemnation rest on them. God's judgment, both in this life and in the life to come, is based on this gospel testimony.

85. Q. HOW IS THE KINGDOM OF HEAVEN CLOSED AND OPENED BY CHRISTIAN DISCIPLINE?

A. According to the command of Christ: Those who, though called Christians, profess unchristian teachings or live unchristian lives, and after repeated and loving counsel refuse to abandon their errors and wickedness, and after being reported to the church, that is, to its officers, fail to respond also to their admonition—such persons the officers exclude from the Christian fellowship by withholding the sacraments from them, and God Himself excludes them from the kingdom of Christ. Such persons, when promising and demonstrating genuine reform, are received again as members of Christ and of His church.

The Keys of the Kingdom

*B*efore I joined the church in fourth grade, I had to meet with the elders and go through the Heidelberg Catechism with my pastor. I read through the whole Catechism and studied it as best I could (or, at least pretty diligently for a nine-year-old). For some reason the only Lord's Day I remember being specifically quizzed on was this one about the keys of the kingdom. I think I remember being tested on it because I remember studying it. And I remember studying it because I had never heard of this terminology before and it sounded pretty cool.

I should have been more familiar with the language because it comes right from Jesus: "I will give you the keys of the kingdom of heaven, and whatever you bind on earth shall be bound in heaven, and whatever you loose on earth shall be loosed in heaven" (Matt. 16:19). The imagery is straightforward: Entrance into the kingdom of heaven—coming under the reign and rule of God in this life and in the life to come—is through the narrow door (cf. Luke 13:24) and this door swings both ways. The kingdom can be opened and the kingdom can be closed.

With so much, everything in fact, riding on our entrance into the kingdom, we would do well to know how the door is opened and closed. The Catechism mentions two keys of the kingdom: preaching and discipline.

Preaching opens the kingdom by proclaiming the gospel. Reformed Christians must not fall into the unbiblical trap of thinking that just because God elects we have no obligation to share the gospel. As Spurgeon once remarked, he preached the gospel, even as a Calvinist, because the elect do not have yellow stripes down their backs. In other words, preachers must offer a free invitation to all to come to Christ for the forgiveness of their sins. True, no one can come unless the Father draws them (John 6:44). But we must also be clear that no one who comes to Christ in true faith will ever be cast out (John 6:37). As the Canons of Dort put it so beautifully: "Moreover, it is the promise of the gospel that whoever believes in Christ crucified shall not perish but have eternal life. This promise, together with the command to repent and believe, *ought to be announced and declared without differentiation or discrimination to all nations and people*, to whom God in his good pleasure sends the gospel" (II.5, emphasis mine). Preachers must never allow their pulpit ministry to devolve into nothing but helpful tips, good advice, and moral exhortation. We are charged with a more solemn task, to open the gates of heaven and call sinners to believe in Christ and receive all His gospel promises.

Likewise, we preachers must not neglect our responsibility to close the kingdom. This is where so much of contemporary preaching fails miserably. Too many of our churches are like the false prophets of old, crying "Peace, peace," where there is no peace. We have scores of people in our congregations, let alone the world, who have never heard of their need to repent, never heard of God's anger against sin, never heard of the judgment to come. If preachers fail to proclaim this message—out of embarrassment, cultural convenience, or just plain biblical ignorance—they are not simply off the mark, they are being unfaithful to their calling as God's ambassadors. Worse, they are unfaithful to the Word of God itself. If we are truly proclaiming the whole counsel of God, we will be an aroma of life to some and the stench of death to others (2 Cor. 2:15–16).

The second key of the kingdom is church discipline. Although discipline is scarcely practiced anymore, there is no doubt about its biblical mandate. Paul in 1 Corinthians 5 and Jesus in Matthew 18 (to name just the most famous examples) make clear that the church has God-given authority to discipline its members. The purpose of discipline is not retribution and the motivation must never be personal animosity. God gives Christian discipline to the church to promote its purity, benefit the offender, and vindicate the honor of the Lord Jesus Christ (RCA Book of Church Order).

Whereas preaching looses and then binds, the nature of discipline is to bind and then loose. Discipline binds, or closes the kingdom, by excluding from church fellowship those who call themselves Christian but repeatedly, after much warning, refuse to abandon their wicked deeds. Discipline is not for light offenses, and certainly not for those who confess their sin and turn from it. Discipline is for those who, because of long seasons of unfruitfulness, give the church and its leaders no choice but to conclude, "This is a bad tree, bearing nothing but bad fruit." Discipline serves as a kind of foretaste of future judgment. If the hardness of heart continues, there will be a worse judgment to come, one that proves that any initial profession of faith in the church member was not genuine.

In making such a judgment (under Christ's authority, not our own), the church's goal and hope is always for repentance. We trust that if the sinner is sincerely a child of God, the discipline will only be for a season and that later the wandering one will return to the narrow path (Heb. 12:5–11). In other words, the hope in binding is that we may later loose. Just as the door to the kingdom is closed through church discipline, so the door is gladly opened again upon confession of sin and evidence of genuine reform. The keys of the kingdom aren't given for power trips. They are given so that in opening the door, many may walk in, and in closing the door, many would be duly warned and seek the only door that leads to eternal life.

86. Q. WE HAVE BEEN DELIVERED FROM OUR MISERY BY GOD'S GRACE ALONE THROUGH CHRIST AND NOT BECAUSE WE HAVE EARNED IT: WHY THEN MUST WE STILL DO GOOD?

A. To be sure, Christ has redeemed us by His blood. But we do good because Christ by His Spirit is also renewing us to be like Himself, so that in all our living we may show that we are thankful to God for all He has done for us, and so that He may be praised through us. And we do good so that we may be assured of our faith by its fruits, and so that by our godly living our neighbors may be won over to Christ.

87. Q. CAN THOSE BE SAVED WHO DO NOT TURN TO GOD FROM THEIR UNGRATEFUL AND IMPENITENT WAYS?

A. By no means. Scripture tells us that no unchaste person, no idolater, adulterer, thief, no covetous person, no drunkard, slanderer, robber, or the like is going to inherit the kingdom of God.

Shall We Sin That Grace May Abound?

With this Lord's Day, we begin the third major section of the Heidelberg Catechism—after *guilt* and *grace*, now comes *gratitude*. One of the major objections to the Christian view of salvation, especially in its Reformed expression, is that salvation by grace alone through faith alone leads to moral license. If we can't earn one tiny iota of deliverance from sin by our good works, then why do good at all?

The catechism gives five reasons in Answer 86. First, we do good because the Holy Spirit is working in us to make us more like Jesus (2 Cor. 3:18). The same Spirit who caused us to be born again and enabled us to believe will also work to make us holy (Rom. 6:9–11). Second, we do good out of gratitude (Rom. 12:1–2). This is not to suggest that God saves us and then we work the rest of our lives to pay Him back for the favor (Rom. 11:33–36). Rather, we do good because the wonder of our salvation produces such thankfulness in our hearts that it is our pleasure to serve God. Third, we do good so that God might be praised by the works we display in His name. "By this my Father is glorified," Jesus said, "that you bear much fruit and so prove to be my disciples" (John 15:8). Fourth, we do good so that we can be assured of our right standing before God. Faith alone justifies, but the faith that justifies is never alone. By bearing good fruit, we show that we are a good tree (Matt. 7:15–20) and make our calling and election sure (2 Peter 1:10). Fifth, we do good in order that we might adorn the gospel (Titus 2:10) and make it attractive to outsiders (1 Peter 2:12).

The Bible is not indifferent to good works. Christians who live in habitual, unrepentant sin show themselves not to be true Christians. Of course, we all stumble (James 3:2; 1 John 1:8). But there's a difference between falling into sin and jumping in with both feet. It doesn't matter the sin—pride, slander, robbery, covetousness, or sexual immorality—if we give ourselves to it and live in it with joyful abandon, we will not inherit the kingdom of God. Simply put, people walking day after day in the same sin without a fight or repentance go to hell (1 Cor. 6:9–10; Gal. 5:19–21; 1 John 3:14).

In our day, careful attention needs to be paid to the issue of sexual immorality in particular. This isn't because Christians are prudes or like to judge others. We have to talk about sexual sin for the simple fact that more and more people, many of them inside the church, sadly refuse to call sexual immorality sin. For the church to be silent on the most important ethical matters of the day is irresponsible and cowardly. This includes same-sex sexual behavior—homosexuality.[38]

We know from Romans 1; Leviticus 18 and 20; 1 Timothy 1; the book of Jude—and the passage from 1 Corinthians 6 partially quoted in Answer 87—that same-sex intercourse is a perversion of the created order and offensive to God. And yet, many churches and denominations (to say nothing of state courthouses) are wrestling with the legitimacy of homosexual behavior. My denomination, the Reformed Church in America, has affirmed biblical teaching on this issue, but continues to show ambivalence toward this stance at the same time. Many others face similar situations. (See also the appendix, "Does the Heidelberg Catechism Forbid Homosexual Behavior?") How can Christians talk about sexual immorality in a way that is both true and gracious?

First, we need courage. We need courage to say that unchecked, unrepentant sexual immorality cannot be tolerated in the church. We need courage in our churches and denominations to affirm clearly, not just on paper, but in our preaching and actions, that unchecked, unrepentant sexual immorality is to be lovingly rebuked, not celebrated. Young people especially need courage to stick out like sore thumbs in their schools and teams and winsomely defend the belief that marriage should be between a man and a woman for a lifetime.

Second, we need humility. We need to check our own hearts to make sure our courage does not become hostility, and our love for the Word of God does not become hate for those who disobey it. We need to ask God to show us our blind spots, whether it has to do with divorce, or greed, or self-righteousness. We need to repent of gay jokes. We need to repent of our own sexual sins.

Third, we need love. We need less rage and more tears. We need less talk about taking back America and more talk about the grace God extends to all sinners. We need to be willing to touch—emotionally, socially, and physically—those who sin just like us, even if they sin in different ways than some of us. We need to love enough to suffer with those who suffer.

Fourth, we need hope. We need hope that God can change the hardest heart and slowly, over time, change the deepest addictions, habits, and orientations. We need to offer hope—the hope of God's mercy, the hope of forgiveness, the hope of eternal life, the hope of a warm, truth-filled, grace-saturated church community, the hope of 1 Corinthians 6:11 that "such *were* some of you."

Finally, we need prayer. Pray that the old mainline denominations would not do the easy thing and try to make all sides happy, but do the hard, loving thing and call sin, sin so that grace can be grace and God can show Himself to be the sort of God who forgives our iniquities, redeems our life from the pit, and satisfies us with good. Pray for those who struggle with sexual temptation, whether it be pornography, lust, or same-gender attraction. Pray that our church would be a welcoming place for strugglers, sinners, and sufferers. Pray for those in the gay community—one of the least-reached people groups on earth—that they would be soft to the gospel and we would be ready to love and share the gospel with them. Pray that God would rid us of unrighteous anger, cowardice, compromise, and fear. And pray that the precious, holy, merciful name of Jesus would be hallowed.

88. Q. WHAT IS INVOLVED IN GENUINE REPENTANCE OR CONVERSION?

A. Two things: the dying-away of the old self, and the coming-to-life of the new.

89. Q. WHAT IS THE DYING-AWAY OF THE OLD SELF?

A. It is to be genuinely sorry for sin, to hate it more and more, and to run away from it.

90. Q. WHAT IS THE COMING-TO-LIFE OF THE NEW SELF?

A. It is wholehearted joy in God through Christ and a delight to do every kind of good as God wants us to.

91. Q. WHAT DO WE DO THAT IS GOOD?

A. Only that which arises out of true faith, conforms to God's law, and is done for His glory; and not that which is based on what we think is right or on established human tradition.

Dying Away and Coming to Life

*C*onversion is essential to the gospel. The world needs to learn and we frequently need to be reminded that Christianity is not about refurbishing a few morals here, or helping you find your own unique spiritual journey there, or simply trying to get you to agree to a few theological statements. We need to be converted.

The Bible talks about conversion in many different ways. Conversion means turning from vain things to serve the living God (Acts 14:15). It means repentance toward God and faith in Jesus Christ (Acts 20:21). Conversion is described as being born again (John 3; 1 Peter 1), as being resurrected with Christ into a new life (Rom. 6:3–4), as being a new creation (James 1:18), as regeneration (Titus 3:5), and as putting off old clothes and putting on new clothes (Col. 3:9–10). Conversion means a change of ownership, from slaves of sin to slaves of righteousness (Rom. 6:17–18) and a change of spiritual status from death to life (John 5:24), and a change from darkness to light (1 Peter 2:9).

The Heidelberg Catechism summarizes the change in conversion by pointing to two realities that happen in genuine repentance: the dying away of the old self (known as *mortification*) and the coming to life of the new (known as *vivification*).

Dying to our old self entails three things. *First, we are sorry for our sin.* We see the foolishness of our ways and regret our choices. *Second, we hate our sin more and more.* It is one thing to feel bad following the repercussions for some action. It is another thing to actually hate our sin and hate it more each day—not just because of the bad consequences it brings us but because of its offensiveness before God (Ps. 51:4). It's not

enough to grit our teeth and do the "right thing" because we fear the repercussions of doing otherwise. We must see the vileness of sin and detest it.
Third, we run away from our sin. Too often, we think that regretting a
past mistake or saying we're sorry for some offense is all that repentance
requires. But true repentance involves a change, putting our old ways
behind us and walking in a different direction (2 Cor. 7:10). We are frequently content with mere talk—talk about how sorry we are, talk about
how rotten we are, talk about how bad our sins are. This is all well and good,
but the last time I checked we are called to "put to death the deeds of the
body," not to merely complain about them (Rom. 8:12–13). We have not
really repented if we are only stirred, but not changed.

The second aspect of true repentance or conversion is the coming to
life of the new self. Notice that the dying away of the old self involved
things like regret and hatred, while coming to life of the new self is described
with words like *joy* and *delight*. Conversion is not simply a new way of
living—though it leads to that. Conversion is a new way of *thinking* and
feeling. It means we behold Christ in a new way, so that He looks clear
where He had been confusing, brilliant where He had been bland, and
supremely glorious where He had been just another regular, slightly above
average guy.

Having our eyes opened to Christ's divine and supernatural light means
more than just a twinge of conscience or being moved with pity at Jesus'
suffering. As Jonathan Edwards says, true converting grace imparts "a real
sense of the excellency of God, and Jesus Christ, and of the work of redemption, and the ways and works of God revealed in the gospel."[39] When the
Spirit of God brings us to life in Christ, He operates on the mind, the
will, *and* the affections. We not only think differently and act differently,
we also feel differently, so that we can truly say, "I've tasted and seen that
the Lord is good" (Ps. 34:8).

In short, conversion brings newness. New life. New direction. New
inclination. New affections. The old has gone and the new has come. In
conversion, the Spirit of God gives us a new awareness of sin, a new interest in the Word of God, a new passion for holiness, a new desire for prayer,
and a new sense of the majesty of God.

This means we obey not because we are slaves bound to our master's will, but because we have been set free and are now at liberty to do what we ought. At times, people may be able to be scared into temporary law keeping. But true conversion goes deeper and affects the heart, making us happy to walk in God's ways and do what is good.

But what, asks the Catechism, is truly "good"? For most people, good deeds are simply those that help people or society in some way. So we figure we have no shortage of good deeds—after all, we recycle, build houses with Habitat for Humanity, give to the American Red Cross, and take our kids on fun vacations. But God's standard is higher and deeper. Good deeds are only those that (1) arise out of true faith (John 15:5; Heb. 11:6), (2) conform to God's law (1 Sam. 15:22; Eph. 2:10), and (3) are done for the glory of God (1 Cor. 10:31). This doesn't mean we can't be thankful for the morality and kindness we see in non-Christians. Certainly, most people do nice things for others. But truly good deeds must do more than help people and spring from more than good intentions. Truly good deeds are done in God's strength through faith in Christ, conform to God's revealed will, and aim to make much of God and not us or the ones we serve.

The Word of God must be our standard of goodness, not nice thoughts, nor pleasant smiles, nor the usefulness of charity. We can be thankful for kindness instead of meanness, but true goodness goes deeper into the heart and higher up to God than mere moralism.

*L*ord's Day 34

92. Q. WHAT DOES THE LORD SAY IN HIS LAW?

A. [The Catechism quotes from Exodus 20:1–17, reciting the giving of the Ten Commandments]

93. Q. HOW ARE THESE COMMANDMENTS DIVIDED?

A. Into two tables. The first has four commandments, teaching us what our relation to God should be. The second has six commandments, teaching us what we owe our neighbor.

94. Q. WHAT DOES THE LORD REQUIRE IN THE FIRST COMMANDMENT?

A. That I, not wanting to endanger my very salvation, avoid and shun all idolatry, magic, superstitious rites, and prayer to saints or to other creatures. That I sincerely acknowledge the only true God, trust Him alone, look to Him for every good thing humbly and patiently, love Him, fear Him, and honor Him with all my heart. In short, that I give up anything rather than go against His will in any way.

95. Q. WHAT IS IDOLATRY?

A. Idolatry is having or inventing something in which one trusts in place of or alongside of the only true God, who has revealed Himself in His Word.

Delighting in the Law
and in the Lord

*T*he Heidelberg Catechism is largely composed of three elements: the Apostles' Creed (Lord's Days 7–22), the Ten Commandments (Lord's Days 34–44), and the Lord's Prayer (Lord's Days 45–52). So even though almost twenty chapters remain in this book, there are only two more topics to cover in the Catechism: the commandments and prayer.

It's worth noting, as many have, that the authors of the Heidelberg Catechism included their exposition of the law in the gratitude section and not the guilt section. This choice reflects the widespread Reformation belief in the so-called third use of the law. The law is given (1) to restrain wickedness and (2) to show us our guilt and lead us to Christ. But, according to Calvin, the "third and principal use" of the law is as an instrument to learn God's will. The law doesn't just show us our sin so we might be drawn to Christ; it shows us how to live as those who belong to Christ.

In one sense Christians are no longer under the law. We are under grace (Rom. 6:14). We have been released from the law (Rom. 7:6) and its tutelage (Gal. 3). On the other hand, having been justified by faith, we uphold the law (Rom. 3:31). Even Christ recoiled at the idea of coming to abolish the law and the prophets (Matt. 5:17). Christians are free from the law in the sense that we are not under the curse of the law; Christ is the end of the law for righteousness to everyone who believes (Rom. 10:4). Nor is the law a nationalized covenant for us like it was for Israel. But the law in general, and the Ten Commandments in particular, still give us a blueprint for how we ought to live.

The Ten Commandments were central to the ethics of the New Testament. Jesus repeated most of the second table of the law to the rich young man (Mark 10:17–22). The apostle Paul repeated them too (Rom. 13:8–10), and used them as the basis for his moral instruction to Timothy (1 Tim. 1:8–11). There can be no doubt that the commandments, even under the new covenant, are holy and righteous and good (Rom. 7:12).

We obey the commandments, therefore, not in order to merit God's favor but out of gratitude for His favor. Don't forget that the Ten Commandments were given to Israel *after* God delivered them from Egypt. The law was a response to redemption, not a cause of it. We must never separate law from gospel. In one sense, the law shows us our sin and leads us to the gospel, but in another sense, the law ought to follow the gospel just as the giving of the Decalogue followed salvation from Egypt. Likewise, Ephesians 2 first explains salvation by grace and then instructs us to walk in the good deeds prepared for us (v. 10). Romans first explains justification and election, and then tells us how to live in response to these mercies (Rom. 12:1). We obey the law in gratitude for the gospel.

The First Commandment establishes biblical religion as an either-or not a both-and proposition. When it comes to choosing whom we will serve as God, there is no middle ground (Josh. 24:15). Jesus was simply reminding His disciples of the First Commandment when He warned them, "No can serve two masters, for either he will hate the one and love the other, or he will be devoted to the one and despise the other" (Matt. 6:24). Israel's problem was always syncretism. They thought they could have the priests and Levites, the tabernacle, the sacrifices, be worshipers of Yahweh, *and* have a little Baal or Asherah or Dagon on the side. It was the *and* that literally killed them.

Loving God is like loving your spouse: When you choose your mate, it is to the exclusion of all others. You can't do both. You can't tell your wife, "Honey, here's my other lover. I really wanted you to meet. I know you'll be great friends. You both mean so much to me." Your wife will say, "It's me or her. You take your pick." No one would think this sort of wife cruel, or proud, or unfair, or intolerant for making such a demand. Monogamy is her right and her husband's promise. The traditional marriage vows includes the phrase "forsaking all others" for a reason, because the nature of the relationship is one of exclusivity. The same is true in our relationship with God. He is jealous for our exclusive commitment.

And don't miss how the First Commandment has been transformed by the coming of Christ. There are two major mountains in the Old and New Testaments—Mount Sinai and the Mount of Transfiguration. The First Commandment, on the other side of the second mount, can only be obeyed by worshiping Jesus. Jesus shows us what the true God is like. He is the one mediator (1 Tim. 2:5). He is the radiance of the glory of God and the exact imprint of His nature (Heb. 1:3). Every knee must bow to Him and every tongue confess that He is Lord (Phil. 2:10). "If you had known me," Jesus said, "you would have known my Father also. From now on you do know him and have seen him" (John 14:7). In other words, when you see the Son, you know the Father. By implication, if you don't know God in Jesus, you don't know God.

The coming of Jesus has changed everything. We cannot speak about God any longer unless we speak of Him as the God and Father of our Lord Jesus Christ. To worship any besides Jesus or to worship God except through Jesus is to commit idolatry. "No one has ever seen God; the only God, who is at the Father's side, he has made him known" (John 1:18).

*L*ord's Day 35

96. Q. WHAT IS GOD'S WILL FOR US IN THE SECOND
COMMANDMENT?

A. That we in no way make any image of God nor worship Him in
any other way than He has commanded in His Word.

97. Q. MAY WE THEN NOT MAKE ANY IMAGE AT ALL?

A. God can not and may not be visibly portrayed in any way.
Although creatures may be portrayed, yet God forbids making or
having such images if one's intention is to worship them or to
serve God through them.

98. Q. BUT MAY NOT IMAGES BE PERMITTED IN THE CHURCHES
AS TEACHING AIDS FOR THE UNLEARNED?

A. No, we shouldn't try to be wiser than God. He wants His people
instructed by the living preaching of His Word—not by idols that
cannot even talk.

A Picture Is
Not Always Worth
a Thousand Words

Some say there is no place for art or sculpting or painting in the Christian life. They cite two prohibitions in the Second Commandment. Number one, we are not to make images that portray God in any form. Number two, we are not to make any pictures or images if our intention is to worship those images or worship God through them. But the artistry in the tabernacle/temple by such craftsmen as Bezalel and Oholiab (see Ex. 35:30–36:4) demonstrates ornamentation and decoration in life is okay, even in places of worship. We don't have to be as plain as possible.

What is wrong is to infuse objects or ornamentations with spiritual efficacy as if these artifacts brought us closer to God, represented God, or established our communion with God.

There are several reasons for the Lord's strong aversion to visible representation. For starters, God is Spirit (John 4:24). He can't be seen. If you make an image of Him to represent Him, you've lost God as He really is, because now you have a visible God instead of an invisible God. Similarly, God is free. Once you have something to represent God or worship as if it were your god, you undermine God's freedom. Idol worshipers think they can bring God with them by carrying a statue. They think they can manage God with rituals or treat Him like a good luck charm (e.g., bringing the ark of the covenant into battle in 1 Sam. 4). And once we think we need an image to get God's attention or that using some artifact demands His attention, we have undercut His freedom.

God is also majestic. His glory cannot be captured in a picture or an image or a form. That's why even in Revelation when we have a vision of the one on the throne, He is "shown" to us in visual metaphors (lightning, rainbow, colors, sea, fire, lamps, thrones, etc.) because His glory is too great to be fully seen.

Finally, God prohibits image worship because He provides His own mediators. The saints in the Old Testament didn't need to fashion an intermediary for themselves. God had already promised to reveal Himself through the prophets, the priestly system, and the Davidic kings. They didn't need statues to mediate God's presence. And if all this was true in the Old Testament, how much more is it true in the New Testament where Jesus is the surest image (*eikon*) of the invisible God (Col. 1:15)?

But what does the Second Commandment really mean for us in the twenty-first century? Let me suggest several points of application. First, I see many dangers in the tradition of iconography that exists in some strands of the church. I'm not saying it is wrong to have a Rembrandt picture of Jesus in your house or a nativity set for Christmas. What's problematic is using pictures of Jesus (or Mary or angels or saints) to focus you in prayer, or statues and icons that you kiss or kneel before in worship, or relics that you infuse with spiritual significance and efficacy. I fail to be convinced by the long-standing arguments that distinguish between worshiping icons and venerating them. Imagine the Israelites explaining to Moses that the golden calf was just an aid in worship or simply an object of veneration. I doubt Moses would have been impressed, nor God for that matter.

Second, we ought to guard against mental images of God. Sometimes Christians are encouraged to "picture God embracing you" or "imagine God running to you with arms wide-open." Granted, as *metaphors*, these may be helpful images to convey God's love for us. But as actual visual pictures in our brains, these images are far less helpful. We should not construe God with a visible image either in carved stone or in our imagination.

Third, we should be cautious in our use of pictures of Jesus. I don't think it is forbidden to draw a picture of Jesus.[40] After all, Jesus made the invisible God visible. He "broke" the Second Commandment. We don't want our kids to be Docetists, thinking of Jesus as being spirit without a real body. But we need to be careful. No one knows for sure what Jesus looked like, so we don't want to assume a certain look in our heads, whether that's a tow-headed, blue-eyed German looking Jesus or the Victorian, high cheek bones, flowing hair, looks-like-He's-wearing-a-dress Jesus. I have no problem with artistic renderings of Jesus, even making Him Indian, Chinese, European, African, or whatever. There is a powerful theological truth conveyed in seeing Jesus depicted with a hundred different ethnicities. But we mustn't think, and our kids must not think, these are actual portraits of the real Jesus.

Finally, we need to be faithful to instruct the people of God. If God designed His people to be taught by the reading and preaching of Holy Scripture, we should not assume that He can't get the job done without images. The argument made during the Reformation was, "We can't lose the images because they are books for the laity. They can't read. They won't understand the faith without them." To which the Reformers replied, "Then we must teach them."

Christianity is a religion where faith comes by hearing (Rom. 10:13–15). Our goal in worship, therefore, is not to entertain or impress the senses but to edify the people by educating them in the Word of God. This is not an excuse for snobbish elitism or impatience with the ignorant. But it means we must devote our energies to teaching people all that Jesus has commanded (Matt. 28:19–20). We cannot capitulate to the contemporary ethos that laments short attention spans and linear thinking. We must resist the urge to get with the spirit of the age and feed our people with more than a steady diet of video clips and sermonettes.

99. Q. WHAT IS GOD'S WILL FOR US IN THE THIRD COM-
MANDMENT?

A. That we neither blaspheme nor misuse the name of God by cursing, perjury, or unnecessary oaths, nor share in such horrible sins
by being silent bystanders. In a word, it requires that we use the
holy name of God only with reverence and awe, so that we may
properly confess Him, pray to Him, and praise Him in everything
we do and say.

100. Q. IS BLASPHEMY OF GOD'S NAME BY SWEARING AND
CURSING REALLY SUCH SERIOUS SIN THAT GOD IS
ANGRY ALSO WITH THOSE WHO DO NOT DO ALL THEY
CAN TO HELP PREVENT IT AND FORBID IT?

A. Yes, indeed. No sin is greater, no sin makes God more angry than
blaspheming His name. That is why He commanded the death
penalty for it.

Out of the Heart
the Mouth Speaks

The Third Commandment forbids taking the Lord's name in vain. God does not want us to empty His name of its meaning or use it in a careless or wicked way.

The Old Testament had a broad catalogue of sins that were seen as violations of the Third Commandment. Blaspheming or cursing the name of God is the most obvious example. (See the story of the son who was stoned to death for blasphemy in Lev. 24). Uttering empty or false oaths were also violations of the Third Commandment (Lev. 19:12; Hos. 10:4), as were giving false visions or false prophecies (cf. Ezek. 13; 21–22). Sorcery, which involved calling on the Lord in an effort to manipulate His power, violated the Third Commandment too (2 Chron. 33:4–7). Strangely enough, sacrificing your children to the god Molech was also viewed as profaning the name of the Lord (Lev. 18:21). The rationale seems to be that if an Israelite were to commit such a heinous sin, he would dishonor the name of Yahweh to whom he had sworn allegiance (cf. Lev. 20:3). Similarly, the Lord's name was considered profaned when priests cut corners in their prescribed sacrifices (Mal. 1:6ff), when the people unlawfully touched holy things (Lev. 22:2), and when they put detestable things in holy places (Jer. 7:30).

Clearly the Third Commandment concerned more than just the use of the tongue. Wherever the people or things that belonged to the Lord were defiled, the Lord—whose name they bore—was also dishonored and the Third Commandment broken.

Historically, the application of the Third Commandment has been very broad too. We see that in Answer 99, where mention is made not just of blaspheming or cursing but also perjury, unnecessary oaths, and standing silently instead of doing all we can to speak against and prevent such actions. Early ethics manuals used the Third Commandment to condemn random Bible direction, improper use of verses, and biblical crossword puzzles. Early Reformed theologians also objected to the use of dice and games of chance by appealing to the Third Commandment. They felt like casting lots was a form of prayer and to be casting lots in a game was calling on the name of God in a vain manner.

We don't need to agree with all of these prohibitions to agree that the Third Commandment speaks to more than just foul language. Of course, it speaks to this issue as well. It says something disturbing about our attitude toward God if we use His name lightly and carelessly. There is no place in the Christian life for using the name of our Creator and Savior as an expression of shock, outrage, or anger. If we are in the habit of letting "Jeez!" and "Oh my God" fly all over the place, we should ask God for better self-control that His name might not be dishonored by our thoughtless language.

The Third Commandment also speaks against vain repetition of the Lord's name. As Jesus reminds us, we are not heard for our many words (Matt. 6:7). We should not babble on like the pagans do, carelessly inserting the Lord's name in our prayers like a comma ("Dear God, we just come to You, God. For, O God, Lord, You're just awesome. God, we need You, Lord. Jesus be with us, Lord God, just help us, Father.") Of course, a sincere heart counts for something, but praying like this does little to reverence God's name.

Moreover, in keeping the Third Commandment, we must not use God's name, to quote Calvin, "for purposes of our own ambition, avarice, or amusement."[41] This means pastors, speakers, and authors must not be peddlers of God's Word, using His name and Word as a plaything for personal profit (2 Cor. 2:17). And it means that a joking, light-hearted approach to the Lord's name is inappropriate. I like humor about Christian idiosyncrasies and the foibles of church culture. But joking about God is another matter entirely. Would you go into a black community on the Martin Luther King Jr. holiday and open up with a joke, "So MLK walks into a bar . . . "? Such an approach, with its flippant attitude to someone special, would be offensive to most of us, just as carelessly tossing around God's name for our amusement is offensive to God.

In addition to these prohibitions, one could also think of many things the Third Commandment requires. We ought to laud God's actions as good, just, and wise, and not profane His name by accusing Him of evil, getting angry at Him. Further, I think it profanes the name of the Lord when out of feminist sensibilities some refuse to call God "our Father," to name Him as He has named Himself.

Finally, we ought to act, think, feel, and speak as is befitting those who are called by the holy name of God. As Christians, we bear the name of Christ. So when we live unholy lives, we besmirch the name by which we are called. People sometimes get real particular that they don't want to be called a "Christian," but insist on "Jesus follower" or "disciples of the Messiah" or something like that. I understand they are trying to distance themselves from unwanted stereotypes, but let's not be ashamed of the name "Christian." It is our family name, and it is biblical (Acts 11:26; 1 Peter 4:16).

So let us exhort one another to live lives that honor the name of Christ our Lord, instead of taking it in vain.

Lord's Day 37

101. Q. BUT MAY WE SWEAR AN OATH IN GOD'S NAME IF WE
DO IT REVERENTLY?

A. Yes, when the government demands it, or when necessity requires
it, in order to maintain and promote truth and trustworthiness for
God's glory and our neighbor's good. Such oaths are approved in
God's Word and were rightly used by Old and New Testament
believers.

102. Q. MAY WE SWEAR BY SAINTS OR OTHER CREATURES?

A. No. A legitimate oath means calling upon God as the one who
knows my heart to witness to my truthfulness and to punish me if
I swear falsely. No creature is worthy of such honor.

Are Oaths Always Wrong?

The Third Commandment is the only commandment that gets two Lord's Days instead of one. And oddly enough, the extra Lord's Day for the Third Commandment deals with an issue that seems rather prosaic. With a hundred other pressing ethical dilemmas to choose from, frankly, the swearing of oaths seems like a pretty poor choice. After all, how often have you heard about Christians reading through the Third Commandment only to stop dead in their tracks, wondering, "But what about swearing oaths!"

Believe it or not, oath-swearing was a hot topic during the Reformation. For starters, the Reformers had to think through their pastoral counsel to ex-Catholics who had made monastic vows, often including the promise of lifelong celibacy, and now wanted to break those vows. Calvin considered these vows, since they were "rash" (i.e., based on future contingencies) and made with the intention of meriting God's favor, to be abominable in God's sight. Hence, they not only could be broken, those who made them were duty bound to repent of making them in the first place.

More important to the Catechism were the vows sworn to saints or angels. Since God alone can know the heart and God is the one who will hold us accountable for matters of the heart, swearing by any other besides Him is an affront to His authority. If you swear "on my mother's grave," you're calling on your mother to vouchsafe for your truthfulness and judge you if you lie. But your mom, no matter how special, is not a searcher of hearts and she is not the Judge. Only God is worthy of such honor (see John 2:24–25; 1 Cor. 2:11; Matt. 10:28). To swear by anyone or anything besides Him is to dishonor His name.

The other more pressing issue during the Reformation was whether oaths were lawful in the first place. The Anabaptist wing of the Reformation believed that Matthew 5:33–37 and James 5:12 forbade the use of any kind of oath. After all, Jesus said, "Do not take an oath at all. . . . Let what you say be simply 'Yes' or 'No'; anything more than this comes from evil" (Matt. 5:34, 37). And yet, the Heidelberg Catechism, like all the magisterial Reformers, defends the use of oaths. Considering Jesus' straightforward teaching on the subject, what justification do we have for swearing oaths, whether before a judge, or in a marriage ceremony, or in private conversation?

First, we need to *look at Jesus' words in context*. Just a few verses earlier, Jesus made clear that He did not come to abolish the law but to fulfill it (Matt. 5:17). His beef is not with the law—which commanded the people to serve God and hold fast to Him, "and by his name you shall swear" (Deut. 10:20)—but with the human traditions added to the law. In particular Jesus is denouncing the common first-century Jewish practice of swearing by something other than God. People would swear by heaven or the earth or by Jerusalem, thinking that this absolved them of the responsibility to keep the oath, since they technically didn't utter God's name. But as Jesus explains, these circumlocutions are nothing but thinly veiled hypocrisy. Heaven is the throne of God, earth is His footstool, and Jerusalem is His city. God is still the judge and searcher of hearts whether you utter His name or not. It's into this context that Jesus says, in effect, "Drop this whole oath business. It's become an exercise in falsehood. Just say what you mean and mean what you say. Enough with all your fancy formulations." Jesus was almost certainly rejecting the manipulation of oaths rather than every kind of oath.

Second, it seems unlikely that Matthew 5 and James 5 were intended as complete prohibitions on all oaths because of how frequently oaths occur in both testaments. Abraham swore to the king of Sodom (Gen. 14:22) and to Abimelech (Gen. 21:24), and Abraham's servant swore to him (Gen. 24:2–9); Jacob swore "by the Fear of his father Isaac" (Gen. 31:53); the leaders of Israel swore to the Gibeonites (Josh. 9:15); Boaz swore to Ruth (Ruth 3:13); and David swore to Bathsheba (1 Kings 1:29–30). Even in the New Testament, we see plenty of oaths. The apostle Paul often called on God as his witness (Rom. 1:9; 9:1; 2 Cor. 1:23; Phil. 1:8; 1 Thess. 2:10). Not only that, Jesus frequently prefaced His statements with the emphatic assurance "truly, truly" and on one occasion swore "by the living God" that He was the Christ (Matt. 26:63–64). And then there's Hebrews 6:13–20, which not only speaks approvingly of people "swear[ing] by something greater than themselves" (v. 16) but highlights God's own oath-taking (v. 13)! How could Jesus have intended to banish all swearing of every kind when we see the propriety of oaths so often in the Scriptures?

Third, oaths, used sparingly and in the right context, can glorify God. To call on "God as my witness" is to call on Him as our superior and judge. In oath-taking, we also confess that God knows the thoughts and intentions of our hearts (Ps. 139:1–6). As one author puts it, "By swearing an oath, we are confessing our faith: God and nobody else, not even ourselves, functions as verifiers of our words."[42]

Reverent oaths can also benefit our neighbors. If everyone could be trusted, there would be no need for oaths. That's why oaths should be virtually unnecessary among Christians. Our word should be our bond. As Christians, we recognize God always knows the hearts whether we call on Him as a witness or not. So in one sense, we are always under an oath to tell the truth. But since we live among truth-dodgers (and are sometimes ourselves), it is necessary and beneficial at times to swear an oath. Our society still respects oaths—whether it's before a judge or at the altar or upon taking public office or by signing your name on some dotted line. Oath-taking promotes the public welfare by encouraging truth telling and holding liars accountable. This is but one example of God's common grace and one way in which Christians can act as leaven in the world and honor the Lord's name all at the same time.

103. Q. WHAT IS GOD'S WILL FOR YOU IN THE FOURTH COMMANDMENT?

A. First, that the gospel ministry and education for it be maintained, and that, especially on the festive day of rest, I regularly attend the assembly of God's people to learn what God's Word teaches, to participate in the sacraments, to pray to God publicly, and to bring Christian offerings for the poor. Second, that every day of my life I rest from my evil ways, let the Lord work in me through His Spirit, and so begin already in this life the eternal Sabbath.

A Festive Day of Rest

The Fourth Commandment is very tricky. It seems like most Christians are either oblivious of the Sabbath and treat it like Saturday interrupted by church, or they advocate a strict Sabbatarianism that tries hard to apply to Sunday the details of the law of Moses (minus the death penalty, of course). Personally, I prefer the simple approach laid out in the Heidelberg Catechism: Go to church on the "festive day of rest" and cease from our evil ways every day of the week. My view is somewhere between "the Fourth Commandment doesn't apply anymore" and "Sunday is the new Sabbath day." This position has the advantage of being middle of the road, which, of course, has the disadvantage of upsetting people on both sides of the road. But, in 1,500 words or fewer, here's my take on the Sabbath.

God created the world with a Sabbath principle. The word "Sabbath" isn't there, but the rest principle is. "God blessed the seventh day and made it holy, because on it God rested from all his work that he had done in creation" (Gen. 2:3). God set aside one day in seven for rest.

Under Moses, the Sabbath principle was central to Israel's identity as God's chosen people. The last command given to Moses before he came down from Mount Sinai instructed the people to "keep the Sabbath, because it is holy for you" (Ex. 31:14). Resting on Saturday was a clear sign of the national covenant with Israel. Under the Mosaic dispensation, the Sabbath was not viewed as a creation ordinance for all humanity but as a sign of the covenant between God and His people. As a sign of the Mosaic covenant, Sabbath-keeping brought blessing for God's people and Sabbath-breaking brought cursing. The Mosaic Sabbath, then, is not identical to the creation Sabbath but builds on its foundation.

Although the day involved numerous regulations and punishments, at the heart of Sabbath-keeping was worship and rest. The Sabbath was "a day of sacred assembly" (Lev. 23:3 NIV) when God's people were set free from their normal labors that they might be free to worship God. The issue was one of trust. The Sabbath reminded Israel of God's sufficiency and supply. Resting one day in seven brought God glory because then He could prove that He was the one responsible for their sanctification, their sustenance, and their salvation (Ezek. 20:11–12; Ex. 16). Sabbath-keeping was a weekly reminder that the Lord was God and they were not.

In the Gospels we see Jesus emphasizing the spiritual significance of the Sabbath. While Jesus certainly kept all of the Mosaic Sabbath commands, He did not hesitate to break the traditions and customs (*Halakah*) of the Jews. He was less concerned about strict Sabbatarianism and more concerned to get to the heart of the Sabbath. For Jesus, the Sabbath was a day of freedom (Luke 13:10–17), a day for healing (Luke 14:1–6), and a day for doing good (Mark 3:1–6).

As we move into the rest of the New Testament, we see that on the one hand there seems to be increasing discontinuity between the Fourth Commandment and what God requires of new covenant Christians. Romans 14:5 says each person should be fully convinced in his own mind whether one day is better than another. This hardly sounds like the kind of Sabbath-keeping enjoined on the Israelites under Moses. More to the point, Colossians 2:17 argues that the Sabbath, along with questions of food and drink and festivals, is "a shadow of the things to come," whose substance is found in Christ.

With texts like these, I don't think there is any escaping the conclusion that we are no longer bound to observe the Jewish Sabbath. As Martin Luther once quipped, "If anywhere the day is made holy for the mere day's sake—if anywhere anyone sets up its observance on a Jewish foundation, then I order you to work on it, to ride on it, to dance on it, to feast on it, to do anything that shall remove this encroachment on Christian liberty."[43] On the other hand, there appears to be continuity between certain *principles* of the Sabbath and early Christian practice. The old Sabbath disappears, but a comparable Lord's Day, in some ways, takes its place.

Clear as mud, right? Well, here's where I come down. By my reckoning, the ceremonial aspect of the Sabbath has been abolished. It has been fulfilled in Christ. The Mosaic covenant was meant to reinforce the creation principle that we must rest from our labors and trust in God. That principle is what we find fulfilled in Christ. Jesus showed us the true meaning of the Sabbath; namely, that we should not rely on ourselves but trust in God as our provider, sustainer, deliverer, and savior. Therefore, I conclude that the binding nature of Sabbath observance has been eliminated.

Having said that, I believe certain principles of Sabbath rest remain and seem to have been quickly appropriated on the Lord's Day. Surprisingly, Calvin did not teach a strict Sabbatarianism like the Westminster divines and the Puritans later would. In commenting on the Fourth Commandment, Calvin wrote, "But, since this commandment has a particular consideration distinct from the others, it requires a slightly different order of exposition. The early fathers customarily called this commandment a foreshadowing because it contains the outward keeping of a day which, upon Christ's coming, was abolished with the other figures. This they say truly, but they touch upon only half the matter. Hence, we must go deeper in our exposition, and ponder three conditions in which, it seems to me, the keeping of this commandment consists."[44] Calvin goes on to ponder three abiding Sabbath principles.

The first Sabbath principle is that it is fitting for one day in seven to be appointed a day set aside for worship. The Sabbath was the Jewish day for worship (Lev. 23:3). In the New Testament, we see that synagogue worship was a regular part of the Jewish Sabbath (Luke 4:16; Acts 13:42–44; 15:21; 17:2; 18:4). After the resurrection, the day for corporate worship for Christians slides from Saturday to Sunday (Acts 20:7; 1 Cor. 16:1–2). Although the Mosaic Sabbath had been abolished in Christ's fulfillment of it, the first Christians did not hesitate to see a new day as being, if not a holy day, then a first among equals. This day was called the Lord's Day (Rev. 1:10) because it was the day our Lord Jesus Christ triumphed over death and the Devil. So they began, where possible, to set aside Sunday as a day specifically for acts of worship.

The second principle is that we trust in Christ enough to rest one day in seven. I don't think we can be very exact about what this means for every Christian everywhere. But I think we see in creation an abiding principle that God made us with the need for rest. Keeping a "Sabbath" not only expresses our trust in God's care, it is also good for us. We all need a day of "get to" not "have to." After all, the Sabbath was made for man and not man for the Sabbath (Mark 2:23–28). So while the legal requirements of the Sabbath have been fulfilled in Christ, I see it as wise that we would set aside one day a week to cease from our labors and rest.

The most explicit and most important Sabbath principle that remains is this: Cease from your works and rest in Christ. We see in Hebrews 4 that God has always offered His people rest—at creation, in the wilderness, in Joshua's day, under David, and still today. There "remains a Sabbath rest for the people of God, for whoever has entered God's rest has also rested from his works as God did from his" (Heb. 4:9–10). Our chief rest is not to turn off the lawn mower on Sunday (though I always do) but to cease from our flawed, sinful works and rest in Christ (Matt. 11:28).

So, yes, we still need to obey the Fourth Commandment (Matt. 5:17). But we need to see how Jesus transforms it. He gives us the substance instead of the shadow. Trust was the point of the Mosaic shadows. But now the substance is here. Sabbath rest is about making Jesus Christ the center of who we are and relying on Him alone for our salvation. It means ceasing to find approval and righteousness in our deeds. It means we stop doubting God's promises and start trusting that spiritual vitality is found only by resting in Him. Keeping the Sabbath means we give up on ourselves and give ourselves over to God, letting the Lord work in us through His Spirit, "and so begin already in this life the eternal Sabbath."

104. Q. WHAT IS GOD'S WILL FOR YOU IN THE FIFTH COM-
MANDMENT?

A. That I honor, love, and be loyal to my father and mother and all
those in authority over me; that I obey and submit to them, as is
proper, when they correct and punish me; and also that I be
patient with their failings—for through them God chooses to rule
us.

Coming of Age and Respecting Authority

*A*dolescent rebellion seems like a rite of passage for families living in twenty-first-century America. In the Old Testament, it was anything but. There was great pressure on parents and children to take the Fifth Commandment seriously. According to Deuteronomic law, if a man had a stubborn and rebellious son who did not obey his parents, though they disciplined him, the parents were to bring him before the elders, publicly denounce their son, and *the parents* presented him before the men of the city where he would be stoned to death (Deut. 21:18–21; cf. Ex. 21:17; Lev. 20:9; Prov. 20:20; 30:11).

Three thousand years later, Calvin explained the harsh punishment with this rationale: "Nature itself ought in a way to teach us this. Those who abusively or stubbornly violate parental authority are monsters, not men! Hence the Lord commands that all those disobedient to their parents be put to death. For since they do not recognize those whose efforts brought them into the light of day, they are not worthy of its benefits."[45] Honoring our parents is not an option reserved just for those who actually like Mom and Dad.

Of course, obedience has its limits. Authority can be abused and parents can make nefarious commands. Acts 5:29 teaches us that we should "obey God rather than men." So clearly if your parents command of you what God forbids or they forbid what God commands, you cannot and must not obey your parents.

While parental authority is not absolute, our problem in American culture is not knee-jerk obedience to parents but a lack of respect for parents and our elders in general. We consider it a given that teenagers rebel. They do sometimes. I pray mine won't, but who knows? But let's not assume it must happen or that it is good when it does. Independence, learning to think for oneself, trying and failing sometimes—these are steps toward adulthood. But stubbornness, rebellion, and disobedience need not be.

It's not the right of American teenagers to break the Fifth Commandment, no matter what their friends or hormones tell them. Never before has our cultural ethos done more to allow for and encourage youthful immaturity. Kids are coddled and their preferences catered to, in the home and in the society at large. Contrary to the fears of some, most households are less patriarchy and more kindergarchy.

Sadly, with the reign of youth-ism comes a disrespect for older generations. Instead of thinking, "This person is older and probably has something to teach me that I don't know yet," we figure, "This person is old and out of date and funny looking and weak and is best ignored." Older folks deserve better, especially Mom and Dad. Even into old age we must honor our parents. We should visit them, listen to their advice, and see they are well cared for later in life. Honor for parents has no statute of limitations.

When we leave the home to establish a place of our own, we can still honor our parents by considering their advice. For example, consider the issue of parental consent prior to marriage. The men of my generation, more than my parents' generation, seem eager to ask for explicit permission from the future father-in-law before popping the question.[46] I happen to think this is a good idea and shows biblical respect for a father's authority, but the fact that so many Christians have approached the matter differently makes me cautious to demand the awkward "talk to her dad" conversation as a prerequisite to marriage (though I always encourage it). Nor do I think parental non-blessing constitutes automatic veto power for every proposed marriage. Parents can object for terrible reasons. (He comes from a poor family, she's a Christian, etc.). And while we sometimes speak wistfully of arranged marriages (which can work out wonderfully), they can be equally disastrous. Having said all that, my counsel to couples has always been to seek their parents' blessing, listen to what they say, show great patience, and be willing to delay the marriage for the sake of further communication.

There is a long tradition of interpreting the Fifth Commandment as speaking more broadly to all positions of authority. All the catechisms and confessions of the Reformation, for example, treated the command to honor father and mother as applicable to other "authority-subordinate" relationships. Indeed, we see clearly from the rest of Scripture that we should honor those to whom honor is due: slaves to masters (Eph. 6:5), wives to husbands (Eph. 5:22), the church to its leaders (Heb. 13:7), younger men to older men (1 Peter 5:5), and citizens to their governing authorities (Rom. 13:1ff.).

No matter which political party is in power, the command is the same: "Honor the king," even as we fear God (1 Peter 2:17 NIV). We must remember that our standard for honoring those in authority is higher than what we hear from some pundits on both sides of the aisle. We would do better to be like David toward Saul, who dared not lay a hand on God's anointed, though the king was a cowardly rascal. In a democracy we have freedom of speech and assembly, and part of how we respect the governing authorities is by trying to lawfully change the governing authorities. There is nothing wrong with strong disagreement and working for change. But we must always honor those over us with our prayers and our respect.

I doubt many of us regularly feel convicted by the Fifth Commandment, but we probably should. How are we really doing? Do we joyfully submit to parents, husbands, and the rule of law? Are we patient with pastors and senators and middle managers? Do we give glad respect to denominational executives, committee chairpersons, and department heads? Do we take care of our aging parents without grumbling and complaining? Do we ever consider their feelings and desires above our own when making plans for the holidays? Would we be happy if our young children treated us like we, now grown, treat our parents?

Jesus was subject to His father and mother (Luke 2:51) when they were imperfect and He was perfect. So surely we can be subject to imperfect people too and honor those granted by God to have authority over us.

105. Q. WHAT IS GOD'S WILL FOR YOU IN THE SIXTH COMMANDMENT?

A. I am not to belittle, insult, hate, or kill my neighbor—not by my thoughts, my words, my look or gesture, and certainly not by actual deeds—and I am not to be party to this in others; rather, I am to put away all desire for revenge. I am not to harm or recklessly endanger myself either. Prevention of murder is also why government is armed with the sword.

106. Q. DOES THIS COMMANDMENT REFER ONLY TO KILLING?

A. By forbidding murder God teaches us that He hates the root of murder: envy, anger, vindictiveness. In God's sight all such are murder.

107. Q. IS IT ENOUGH THEN THAT WE DO NOT KILL OUR NEIGHBOR IN ANY SUCH WAY?

A. No. By condemning envy, hatred, and anger God tells us to love our neighbors as ourselves, to be patient, peace-loving, gentle, merciful, and friendly to them, to protect them from harm as much as we can, and to do good even to our enemies.

Getting Away with Murder

he Sixth Commandment prohibits the taking of innocent human life. There are two fundamental reasons for this prohibition: (1) our solidarity with the human race (i.e., love your neighbor as yourself) and (2) the inherent worth and dignity of every human being by virtue of being created in the image of God (Gen. 1:26–27; 9:5–6). You don't tackle the players wearing your same jersey, and you don't kill the person who wears the same image of God.

Some of the older translations read, "Do not kill," but "murder"— as newer translations have it—is more accurate. The Hebrew word *ratsach* used in Exodus 20:13 occurs mostly in the few passages, that talk about cities of refuge for those who unintentionally murder (what we would call involuntary manslaughter). Outside of these passages it occurs maybe a dozen times, while *qatal* (to kill) occurs literally hundreds of times. *Qatal* is the general word; *ratsach* the more specific. In short, the Sixth Commandment does not prohibit killing of every kind but only murder.

The Sixth Commandment forbids intentional premeditated murder, intentional unpremeditated murder, reckless homicide (i.e., involuntary manslaughter), and negligent homicide (Judg. 20:4; 1 Kings 21:19; Deut. 22:8; Ex. 21:28–29). But there are other kinds of killing, in specific contexts, that were not forbidden in the Bible: self-defense (Ex. 22:2–3), capital punishment (Gen. 9:6; cf. 2 Sam. 12:9–10; 1 Kings 21:19; Rom. 13:4), and just war (besides all the Old Testament examples of warfare, see Rom. 13:1ff and the way Jesus and John the Baptist respond to soldiers in Luke 7:1–10 and 3:14).

It's worth mentioning that in the Old Testament abortion was also considered a violation of the Sixth Commandment. Besides the familiar verse from Psalm 139 about being knit together in our mother's womb, we have Exodus 21 (explaining the Decalogue from Exodus 20) where retribution (eye for eye, tooth for tooth) is mandated for anyone who injures a pregnant woman's baby (vv. 22–25).

The church, until very recently, has universally opposed abortion. The first- or second-century church manual, *The Didache*, included the commandment: "Do not murder a child by abortion or kill a newborn infant."[47] Likewise Calvin argued passionately that "the fetus, though enclosed in the womb of its mother, is already a human being, and it is almost a monstrous crime to rob it of the life which it has not yet begun to enjoy."[48] Tragically, since 1973 and the U.S. Supreme Court's ruling in *Roe v. Wade*, America has had one of the most permissive abortion policies in the world. Even though fetal homicide laws in most states punish those who injure or kill a child in utero, the destruction of the same child in hospitals and Planned Parenthood clinics is allowed for any reason. As Romans puts it, "They show that the work of the law is written on their hearts, while their conscience also bears witness, and their conflicting thoughts accuse or even excuse them" (2:15).

The Catechism, however, does not talk about abortion, or capital punishment, or just war theory. The authors of the Heidelberg Catechism were not faced with these ethical dilemmas in their day. So they used the Sixth Commandment to talk about the heart. As Jesus makes clear in the Sermon on the Mount, murder is not the only thing forbidden here (Matt. 5:21–22). The commandment also teaches that God hates the root of murder: envy, anger, vindictiveness, and any thoughts, words, looks, or deeds that insult or belittle our neighbor. What's more, "God tells us to love our neighbors as ourselves, to be patient, peace-loving, gentle, merciful, and friendly to them, to protect them from harm as much as we can, and to do good even to our enemies" (Q/A 107).

This is where the commandment gets tough. I've never performed an abortion or committed involuntary manslaughter (though there is forgiveness for both), but I struggled with unrighteous anger just yesterday. I grimaced as the car in front of me went 55 mph instead of 70, and I growled as my children bounced off the walls instead of bounding into bed. These are not made-up examples. I really do get angry, usually unrighteously so. And it's not funny; it's a sin.

Anger is one of those respectable sins. It doesn't seem like a big deal. Granted, not all anger is sin (think Jesus in the temple). It is possible to be angry and sin not (Eph. 4:26). But, honestly, that doesn't describe most of our anger. Sinful anger is anger directed at the wrong person, motivated by the wrong reasons, or out of proportion to the offense. Sadly, this is a truer description of our anger. We take our rage out on other people, get upset for less than noble purposes, and blow up over minor hurts and slight inconveniences. We get grumpy with checkout clerks, snap at tech support over the phone, hold grudges against our spouse, spew venom when sports don't go our way, wish the worst on our enemies, and cherish thoughts of revenge toward those who hurt us.

We have an anger problem. And we don't just *get* frustrated or get our buttons *pushed*; people don't *make* us angry or *make* us lose our cool. We *are* angry. Anger, whatever else may stir it up, comes from an angry heart. And this is no small problem. Anger gives opportunity to the Devil (Eph. 4:27). Hatred is considered murder and no murderer has eternal life abiding in him (1 John 3:15). Strife, fits of anger, and dissensions are works of the flesh and those who do such things will not inherit the kingdom of God (Gal. 5:19–21).

I'm all for passion and righteous indignation. I want people who hate injustice and despise falsehood. But I don't want a church full of mean, angry people. We are to love our enemies and pray for those who persecute us. If we only love those who love us, "what reward do [we] have? Do not even tax collectors do the same?" (Matt. 5:46; cf. v. 44)

We can talk about murder and the sins of others, but if we do not love our neighbors—even those who get their theology all wrong and those who annoy us to no end—we have not been transformed by the Spirit of Jesus and we have not truly understood the Sixth Commandment.

*L*ord's Day 41

108. Q. WHAT IS GOD'S WILL FOR YOU IN THE SEVENTH COMMANDMENT?

A. God condemns all unchastity. We should therefore thoroughly detest it and, married or single, live decent and chaste lives.

109. Q. DOES GOD, IN THIS COMMANDMENT, FORBID ONLY SUCH SCANDALOUS SINS AS ADULTERY?

A. We are temples of the Holy Spirit, body and soul, and God wants both to be kept clean and holy. That is why He forbids everything which incites unchastity, whether it be actions, looks, talk, thoughts, or desires.

Swords for the Fight
Against Lust

*I*s there any command more ridiculed in our culture than the Seventh Commandment? Adultery is a joke; homosexuality is a right; sex before marriage is the norm; no-fault divorce and remarriage is assumed; bestiality is increasingly considered avant garde. This is the world we live in. Sex has always been a leading vote-getter in the most popular sin contest, but never before in this country has so much sexual deviance been made to look so normal and God's standards made to look so obscene.

Our lives are awash in sexuality. Sex is on the television, in the movies, in our music, on the side of buses, and in our books. We can hardly avoid it during halftime shows and in glossy close-ups at supermarket checkouts. Sex is all around us in the mall, dripping off every beer commercial, and two stories high on our billboards.

And of course, sex is on the Internet. Pornography and sex-related sites make up 60 percent of daily web traffic. Of Internet users in the United States, 40 percent visit porn sites at least once a month, and that number increases to 70 percent when the audience is eighteen- to thirty-four-year-old males. Among children ages eight to sixteen with Internet access, 90 percent have viewed pornography online, and the average age of exposure is eleven.[49] The Seventh Commandment is not just broken in this country; it's being smashed to pieces.

None of us is immune from the dangers of sexual immorality. In a 2000 *Christianity Today* study, 40 percent of clergy acknowledged visiting pornographic websites. Yet another survey at Pastors.com found that 50 percent of pastors reported viewing pornography in the previous year.[50] And then there's the underlying issue of the heart. The Seventh Commandment doesn't just forbid adultery and pornography. It forbids every action, look, conversation, thought, or desire that incites lust and uncleanness.

So how can we, with our sex-saturated hearts, obey the Seventh Commandment? Let me suggest twelve passages of Scripture that can help us fight lust and the temptation to sexual immorality.

(1) Lamentations 3:25–27: *"The Lord is good to those who wait for him, to the soul who seeks him. It is good that one should wait quietly for the salvation of the Lord. It is good for a man that he bear the yoke in his youth."* This verse is for singles (including women). Granted, this passage isn't talking about waiting for a spouse. It's about waiting on the Lord. But that's the point. The Lord is good to those who wait for Him. He knows what you need. The preceding verses tell us, "The steadfast love of the Lord never ceases, his mercies never come to an end; they are new every morning; great is your faithfulness. The Lord is my portion, says my soul, therefore I will hope in him." Don't think, *How can I live without sex for another year or decade or two decades?* Think about today. The Lord has given you grace for this day, and He will give you grace for the next sexless, spouseless day.

(2) Proverbs 5:18–19: *"Let your fountain be blessed, and rejoice in the wife of your youth, a lovely deer, a graceful doe. Let her breasts fill you at all times with delight; be intoxicated always in her love."* This may seem a strange text for fighting sexual temptation, but married couples need to know they have delight at their lawful disposal. We need to know that sex is good, intimacy is good, bodies together in marriage are good. Good, glorious sex is spiritual warfare for the married couple.

(3) James 1:14–15: *"But each person is tempted when he is lured and enticed by his own desire. Then desire when it has conceived gives birth to sin, and sin when it is fully grown brings forth death."* This passage helps us understand how temptation works and reminds us that feeling tempted is not the same as sinning. Temptation is an enticement or allurement. That's not sin. When the desire is nurtured, it conceives and gives birth to sin (sin in the flesh or sin in the mind). Sin then grows and matures and leads to death. It is not lust to be attracted to someone or notice he or she is good-

looking. It is not lust to have a strong desire for sex. It is not lust to be excited
about sex in marriage. It is not lust to experience sexual temptation. It's sin
to take another look and mull over the thought for awhile. Just ask King
David.

(4) Romans 14:21: *"It is good not to eat meat or drink wine or do anything that causes your brother to stumble."* As Christians, we want to help
each other avoid sin, not lead one another into it with flirting, coarse
joking, and immodest dress.

(5) Matthew 5:27–30: *"You have heard that it was said, 'You shall not
commit adultery.' But I say to you that everyone who looks at a woman with
lustful intent has already committed adultery with her in his heart. If your
right eye causes you to sin, tear it out and throw it away. For it is better that
you lose one of your members than that your whole body be thrown into hell.
And if your right hand causes you to sin, cut it off and throw it away. For it
is better that you lose one of your members than that your whole body go into
hell."* We don't "thoroughly detest" sin (Q/A 108). We make excuses. We
don't get radical. Avoid the movies, get rid of your Internet connection,
don't kiss before marriage, throw out your TV, tear out your eye—whatever it takes to battle lust. There are too many whole-bodied people going
to hell and not enough spiritual amputees going to heaven.

(6) Galatians 6:7: *"Do not be deceived: God is not mocked, for whatever
one sows, that will he also reap."* There are often temporal consequences
for disobedience. It could be STDs, baggage in marriage, a guilty conscience, distraction at work, a pornography fetish you pass on to your
children that destroys your family, your marriage, or your ministry. There
are also eternal consequences if you give yourself over to this sin. "For the
one who sows to his own flesh will from the flesh reap corruption, but the
one who sows to the Spirit will from the Spirit reap eternal life" (Gal. 6:8).

(7) 1 Corinthians 6:15–20: *"Do you not know that your bodies are members of Christ? Shall I then take the members of Christ and make them members of a prostitute? Never! . . . Or do you not know that your body is a temple
of the Holy Spirit within you, whom you have from God? You are not your
own, for you were bought with a price. So glorify God in your body."* We need
a theology of the body: the body is good, but it's not yours. Jesus didn't just
die to ransom our souls. He also died for your body. It belongs to God.

(8) 2 Corinthians 5:17: *"Therefore, if anyone is in Christ, he is a new creation. The old has passed away; behold, the new has come."* Cultural liberalism says, "Just be yourself." Self-help doctrine says, "You can find a better you if you just dig deep enough." Moralism says, "Be a better person." The Bible says, "You are a new person by God's grace, now live like it." "Be who you are" is the gospel motivation for holiness.

(9) Hebrews 10:24–25: *"And let us consider how to stir up one another to love and good works, not neglecting to meet together, as is the habit of some, but encouraging one another, and all the more as you see the Day drawing near."* No one fights a war by himself, and no one will get victory over sexual sin on her own. You need to talk to others about your struggles and listen just as well. Be honest. Ask good questions. Don't just confess and feel better. Repent and change. Don't just sympathize, admonish. Follow up with your brothers and sisters. Pray and remind each other of the gospel.

(10) James 4:6: *"But he gives more grace. Therefore it says, 'God opposes the proud, but gives grace to the humble.'"* God always gives more grace. So keep coming to Him with your sin and all your commandment violations. Confess like David in Psalm 51 that you have sinned against God. Confess that God is the most offended party as a result of your sin.

(11) Matthew 5:8: *"Blessed are the pure in heart, for they shall see God."* This has been the most helpful verse for me in fighting lust and the temptation to sexual immorality. We need to fight desire with desire.[51] Satan tempts us by holding out something that will be pleasurable to us. We aren't tempted to gorge ourselves on liverwurst, because for most it doesn't hold out the promise of great pleasure. But sex does. Pornography does. A second look does. The Bible gives us many weapons to fight temptation. We need to fight the fleeting pleasure of sexual sin with the far greater, more abiding pleasure of knowing God. The fight for sexual purity is the fight of faith. It may sound like nothing but hard work and gritting your teeth, the very opposite of faith. But faith is at the heart of this struggle. Do we believe that a glimpse of God is better than a glimpse of skin? Do we believe that God's steadfast love is better than life (Ps. 63:3)? We'd probably sin less if we spent less time thinking about our sins, sexual or otherwise, and more time meditating on the love and holiness of God.

(12) Ephesians 1:18–21: *"That you may know . . . the immeasurable*

greatness of his power toward us who believe, according to the working of his great might that he worked in Christ when he raised him from the dead and seated him at his right hand in the heavenly places, far above all rule and authority and power and dominion." The great power that created the world, and saved us, and raised Jesus from the dead—that same power is now at work in you. We must believe that God is stronger than sexual temptation, sin, and addiction. If you believe that God brought a dead man back to life, you should believe that you can change. Not overnight, usually, but from one degree of glory to the next.

110. Q. WHAT DOES GOD FORBID IN THE EIGHTH COMMAND-
MENT?

   A. He forbids not only outright theft and robbery, punishable by law.
   But in God's sight theft also includes cheating and swindling our
   neighbor by schemes made to appear legitimate, such as: inaccu-
   rate measurements of weight, size, or volume; fraudulent mer-
   chandising; counterfeit money; excessive interest; or any other
   means forbidden by God. In addition He forbids all greed and
   pointless squandering of His gifts.

111. Q. WHAT DOES GOD REQUIRE OF YOU IN THIS COMMAND-
MENT?

   A. That I do whatever I can for my neighbor's good, that I treat
   others as I would like them to treat me, and that I work faithfully
   so that I may share with those in need.

Justice and Generosity

"You shall not steal" seems like a relatively safe command. We know the Third Commandment is going to trip us up, because we've all lost control of our tongue from time to time. The commands against adultery and murder, when they are considered matters of the heart, are certainly going to bring some conviction. Even the command to rest will probably cause a squirm or two. But the Eighth Commandment seems pretty safe. In one survey by the Barna Research Group, 86 percent of adults claimed they are completely satisfying God's requirement regarding abstinence from stealing.[52]

Look, I don't break into people's homes and I don't shoplift, we think to ourselves. *Finally, I've gotten to a commandment I can feel good about.*

But as the Catechism points out, the Eighth Commandment forbids more than outright theft and robbery. The Eighth Commandment prohibits taking anything that doesn't belong to us. This includes everything from kids swiping toys in the nursery to plagiarism in papers and sermons to online piracy.

You can add chattel slavery to the list. It's true that the Bible regulates slavery and doesn't outlaw it. But some people make it sound like the Bible is one big pro-slavery book. It isn't. In fact, chattel slavery like the kind that prospered in the New World was outlawed in the Bible as a violation of the Eighth Commandment. Exodus 21:16 says, "Whoever steals a man and sells him, and anyone found in possession of him, shall be put to death" (cf. Deut. 24:7). Likewise, 1 Timothy 1:10 denounces "enslavers." The Bible may not condemn every form of slavery, but the images of rounding up Africans and herding them into squalid ships to cross the Atlantic where they would be bought and sold in the New World are images the Bible rejects outright as sin.

The Eighth Commandment forbids injustice of any kind. The Bible has a lot to say about cheating scales and false measures, or any means by which you get more from a transaction than you deserve. One quickly thinks of present-day accounting scandals and ponzi schemes. Especially grievous is swindling the poor, by obvious oppression, or by exploiting a lack of education (think predatory loans), or by making false promises that hurt the people you are claiming to help (think casinos and the lottery). As Luther puts it, "A person steals not only when he robs a man's safe or his pocket, but also when he takes advantage of his neighbor at the market, in a grocery shop, butcher stall, wine-and-beer cellar, work-shop, and, in short, wherever business is transacted and money is exchanged for goods or labor."[53]

The Eighth Commandment is also broken when we are wasteful and lazy. Slacking off at work, fudging expense reports, stealing out of the warehouse, taking money from petty cash, falsifying sign-in sheets, giving merchandise away, writing bottle return slips to yourself—all these rob our employer of his money and are offensive to God.

God laments our slothfulness too. We ought to be "doing honest work with [our] own hands" (Eph. 4:28) and learn to live independently (1 Thess. 4:11–12). When able-bodied men take handouts instead of doing all they can to work, they are robbing from others to feed their own laziness (2 Thess. 3:10).

Finally, and most poignantly, the Eighth Commandment forbids greed—stealing with the eyes of our heart. The biblical view of wealth and possessions is not simple. On the one hand, the poor seemed to be on much safer ground around Jesus than the rich. But on the other hand, we see throughout the Bible examples of godly rich people (Job, Abraham, well-to-do women following Jesus, Joseph of Arimathea).

On the one hand, riches are a blessing from the hand of God (e.g., patriarchs, Mosaic covenant, Proverbs, Kings). But on the other hand, there is almost nothing that puts you in more spiritual danger than money ("How difficult it will be for those who have wealth to enter the kingdom of God!" is how Jesus put it in Mark 10:23).

On the one hand, Jesus and the prophets have very little positive to say about the rich and sympathize more with the poor. On the other hand, God put the first man and woman in a paradise of plenty, and the vision of the new heavens and the new earth is a vision of opulence, feasting, and prosperity.

And then you have the famous "middle-class" passage: "Remove far from me falsehood and lying; give me neither poverty nor riches; feed me with the food that is needful for me, lest I be full and deny you and say, 'Who is the Lord?' or lest I be poor and steal and profane the name of my God" (Prov. 30:8–9). It is impossible to give a one-sentence summary of the Bible's perspective on money.

But it is possible to give a one-sentence summary on what God thinks about loving money. The love of money is a very, very bad thing. "No one can serve two masters, for either he will hate the one and love the other, or he will be devoted to the one and despise the other. You cannot serve God and money" (Matt. 6:24). "For the love of money is a root of all kinds of evils. It is through this craving that some have wandered away from the faith and pierced themselves with many pangs" (1 Tim. 6:10). "Keep your life free from the love of money" (Heb. 13:5). Read Ecclesiastes sometime and you'll see that the love of money does not satisfy, compromises our integrity, produces worry, ruins relationships, provides no lasting security, and does nothing to accomplish anything good for us in eternity. When we are greedy, it is bad for others and worse for ourselves.

The opposite of the love of money is generosity. Instead of hoarding our money, we hand it over. Instead of building bigger barns, we nurture bigger hearts. Instead of looking to take, we seek to give. We who have been given everything—life, food, family, freedom, new birth, forgiveness, redemption, the Holy Spirit, the promise of an unimaginable inheritance—surely ought to give something to those who need our help. Gospel people know that to whom much is given, much is expected.

*L*ord's Day 43

112. Q. WHAT IS GOD'S WILL FOR YOU IN THE NINTH
COMMANDMENT?

A. God's will is that I never give false testimony against anyone, twist
no one's words, not gossip or slander, nor join in condemning
anyone without a hearing or without a just cause. Rather, in court
and everywhere else, I should avoid lying and deceit of every kind;
these are devices the devil himself uses, and they would call down
on me God's intense anger. I should love the truth, speak it candidly, and openly acknowledge it. And I should do what I can to
guard and advance my neighbor's good name.

It Hurts So Good

*O*uch. If you don't feel a little guilty after reading this Lord's Day Q and A, you were reading too fast. I don't consider myself a liar—but, boy, does this Lord's Day hurt. I may not have lied in court, but I have done most everything else listed in Answer 112. Take a closer look and see if your conscience gets pricked.

"Never give false testimony against anyone." Have you ever said a half-truth about someone? Have you ever born false witness to someone's character or ideas? If so, you've broken the Ninth Commandment.

"Twists no one's words." How many times have I retold a story so that I look the hero and everyone else looks like a dolt? How quickly we learn to emphasize the nasty things they said and leave out the hurtful things we said. How easily we can pass along our interpretation of the story as if it were the facts of the story, only to stop short when someone asks, "Is that exactly what she said?"

"Not gossip or slander." We can gossip in one of two ways: by passing a rumor that can't be substantiated or by passing along a true report unnecessarily. Before we share that "prayer request" or reveal something "just between friends," we should ask some questions. Would the person I'm about to talk about be happy for others to know this? If I share this story, what good will come of it? Am I sharing this negative incident about someone else so that I can feel closer to the person I'm talking to? (There is no faster way to make a friend than to find a mutual enemy.) If I tell this bit of news, will it lead the person I'm talking with to form an overly negative view of the other person? Gossip can be deceit even if it is true because it leads people to think worse of others than they should. Even if we preface our remarks with "He's really a good guy" or "God bless him," it can still be gossip. When it comes to juicy information, we should always err on the side of keeping the circle as small as possible. Avoid being "a whisperer" (see Prov. 18:8 ESV, NASB).

If gossip is sharing unsubstantiated or unnecessary information about others, slander is spreading false reports about others. This includes putting the worst possible motives on others' intentions, refusing to ever give the benefit of the doubt, and assuming the worst about people and reporting it to others as fact. Slander also includes allowing people to believe critical things about others when we know the information to be false. Any time we help others believe what is untrue about people, we are contributing to slander.

"Nor join in condemning anyone without a hearing or without a just cause." There is something very biblical about the principle of innocent until proven guilty. Awhile back I was summoned for jury duty. Even though I didn't get seated, I got to hear what the case was about. As I heard the general outline of the case, I found myself immediately thinking, "Well, obviously this guy did *something* wrong." Maybe he did. But to assume so from the outset is to condemn someone without a hearing. It can be hard not to assume that accused athletes are guilty of steroid use or accused politicians are guilty of infidelity. But we should not rush to judgment on anyone.

This doesn't mean we can't make judgments, even very critical judgments, at times. But we should not do so without information. Not without cause. "Judge not, that you be not judged," Jesus said (Matt. 7:1). "With the measure you use it will be measured back to you" (Luke 6:38). We should be hoping people are better than we think, just as we would want others to judge us charitably. The Ninth Commandment, not to mention the law of love, enjoins us not to construe people's words in the worst possible way.

"Rather, in court and everywhere else, I should avoid lying and deceit of every kind." The words "every kind" really get me. How often do we tweak our stories just a tad, exaggerating the amount of snow that fell, or how long we studied, or how fast we ran? I've found myself even wanting to fudge the time I get up in the morning, so that my day sounds a little more impressive. And what about failing to keep our promises—is this not a form of lying and deceit? Everyone forgets appointments once in a while, but nowadays many people will think nothing of breaking their commitments or talking a bigger game than they know they can deliver. "It is better that you should not vow," the Preacher says, "than that you should vow and not pay" (Eccl. 5:5).

The saddest part is that when we lie, in little ways or big ways, we are showing our allegiance to the wrong father. Lies and deceit "are the devices the devil himself uses, and they would call down on me God's intense anger," Answer 112 tells us. The remedy is to follow the example of our heavenly Father, whose words always prove true (Prov. 30:5). We should, like God, "love the truth, speak it candidly, and openly acknowledge it."

And finally, we should always do what we can "to guard and advance [our] neighbor's good name." Proverbs tells us, "A good name is to be chosen rather than great riches, and favor is better than silver or gold" (22:1). This verse came to mind after I finished reading Clarence Thomas's autobiography a couple of years ago. Thomas, you remember, was barely nominated for the Supreme Court because sexual harassment charges were raised against him. I don't claim to know what really happened, but after reading Thomas's candor about other failings in his life, I couldn't help but believe his profession of innocence. If he was innocent, think of all he has suffered because he lost his good name. Whether we are dealing with our enemies or our friends, the words of the Christian should always defend the truth. "Too many of us delight in a certain poisoned sweetness," as Calvin puts it.

If we truly love our neighbor as ourselves, we will do whatever we can to protect his name.

113. Q. WHAT IS GOD'S WILL FOR YOU IN THE TENTH COMMANDMENT?

   A. That not even the slightest thought or desire contrary to any one of God's commandments should ever arise in my heart. Rather, with all my heart I should always hate sin and take pleasure in whatever is right.

114. Q. BUT CAN THOSE CONVERTED TO GOD OBEY THESE COMMANDMENTS PERFECTLY?

   A. No. In this life even the holiest have only a small beginning of this obedience. Nevertheless, with all seriousness of purpose, they do begin to live according to all, not only some, of God's commandments.

115. Q. NO ONE IN THIS LIFE CAN OBEY THE TEN COMMANDMENTS PERFECTLY: WHY THEN DOES GOD WANT THEM PREACHED SO POINTEDLY?

   A. First, so that the longer we live the more we may come to know our sinfulness and the more eagerly look to Christ for forgiveness of sins and righteousness. Second, so that, while praying to God for the grace of the Holy Spirit, we may never stop striving to be renewed more and more after God's image, until after this life we reach our goal: perfection.

Covetous or Content?

*H*ave you ever stopped to think how easy it is to break the Tenth Commandment, shown in Exodus 20:17?

"You shall not covet your neighbor's house." You visit her home the first time and come away thinking, *Boy, she has a lot of nice stuff. I wish my house could be decorated like hers. I wish I could live in that 3,500-square-foot home and she could live in my 1,200-square-foot hole-in-the-wall. We live in a dump. It's embarrassing. Life must be pretty nice in a house like that.*

"You shall not covet your neighbor's wife." Here comes that thought: *Why did I marry my wife? That other wife over there is always so friendly, and her kids are perfect and their house is always immaculate. Why couldn't my wife have aged like that? I wish I could be married to someone like her.*

"You shall not covet your neighbor's male servant, his female servant, his ox, or his donkey." *It's not fair. All the other families go on great vacations. They go to Disney World. They go see the Grand Canyon. Some of them get to travel to Europe or go on cruises. We just go to Grandma's house or the county fair. I ought to be able to take those vacations just like everybody else.*

"You shall not covet anything that is your neighbor's." Which of these thoughts have you had? *If only I could be smart like him. . . . My life would be so much better if I was shaped like her. . . . Why couldn't I get normal parents, like my friends have? . . . Everything in my life is hard, below average, and poor. Everything in their life is easy, above average, and rich. It shouldn't be this way. Oh, how I wish we were them and they were us.*

The Bible speaks against the sin of covetousness in the strongest terms possible. Without your being sanctified by the Savior, covetousness will keep you out of heaven (Rom. 1:28–29; 1 Cor. 6:9–11). Covetousness is idolatry (Eph. 5:5).

Just to be clear: Coveting is not the same as desire. The Tenth Commandment is not prohibiting any kind of longing or want. One of two things must be present for a lawful desire to become coveting. First, we covet when we desire what belongs to someone else. Coveting is to stealing what lust is to adultery. Sex is good and possessions are good. But sex is bad outside of marriage. And possessions are bad if you take them from someone else. Coveting says, "I want what they have and I don't care if they have it." Coveting is a violation of the second Great Commandment, to love your neighbor like yourself because when we covet we only think of what would be good for us, what we would like, what would make us happy, how our lives could be made better, regardless of how others are affected.

Or we can covet when our desire leads to or is an expression of discontentment. This aspect of coveting has more to do with the first Great Commandment. Some of us don't get jealous when our friend's house looks like Pottery Barn. We don't want to take away what they have. We just want to have it too—then we can be happy as well! If you are frequently complaining about your house, your spouse, the quality or quantity of your possessions, or the general state of your life, you are breaking the Tenth Commandment.

Contentment and covetousness are opposites. Covetousness says, "I need that. I won't be happy without it. It isn't fair; I don't have it. I want that more than anything else." Contentment says, "I have what I need. I am happy in the Lord. He does good to all. I want nothing more than I have." So if you aren't content, you're almost certain coveting.

Mercifully, this section on the Ten Commandments ends with a realistic appraisal of our ability to obey the commandments. "In this life even the holiest have only a small beginning of this obedience." Thank the Lord for that! God does not expect perfection. We botched it today and we'll botch it tomorrow. The Ten Commandments, then, ought to lead us to Christ. They show us our sin and lead us to the cross to find our Savior.

Nevertheless, don't think this is only purpose of the commandments.

We won't obey them fully. Not even close. But this doesn't mean our obedience can't get closer. Just because we will never get 100 percent in the classroom of divine obedience doesn't mean we have to settle for complete failure. We ought to *begin* to live according to these ten commands for holy living. We should strive after the perfect goal, even if we will not reach it on this side of the celestial city.

116. Q. WHY DO CHRISTIANS NEED TO PRAY?

A. Because prayer is the most important part of the thankfulness God requires of us. And also because God gives His grace and Holy Spirit only to those who pray continually and groan inwardly, asking God for these gifts and thanking Him for them.

117. Q. HOW DOES GOD WANT US TO PRAY SO THAT HE WILL LISTEN TO US?

A. First, we must pray from the heart to no other than the one true God, who has revealed Himself in His Word, asking for everything He has commanded us to ask for. Second, we must acknowledge our need and misery, hiding nothing, and humble ourselves in His majestic presence. Third, we must rest on this unshakable foundation: even though we do not deserve it, God will surely listen to our prayer because of Christ our Lord. This is what He promised us in His Word.

118. Q. WHAT DID GOD COMMAND US TO PRAY FOR?

A. Everything we need, spiritually and physically, as embraced in the prayer Christ our Lord Himself taught us.

119. Q. WHAT IS THE PRAYER?

A. Our Father in heaven, hallowed be Your name, Your kingdom come, Your will be done on earth as it is in heaven. Give us today our daily bread. Forgive us our debts, as we also have forgiven our debtors. And lead us not into temptation, but deliver us from the evil one. For Yours is the kingdom and the power and the glory forever. Amen.

The Why, How, What of Prayer

The Catechism asks three questions to help us get to the heart of prayer.

First, *why* does God want us to pray? That's not a dumb question. If God is sovereign such that everything comes to us from His fatherly hand (chap. 10), why would we even need to pray? Doesn't God have everything figured out already?

Well, we don't pray because God needs help running the universe. We don't pray to change God's mind. We pray out of gratitude. We talk to God to praise Him for all the good He has done for us. We talk to Him because we are privileged to belong to Him. Imagine you got down on your knee and proposed to a special young lady. You know she's way out of your league, but amazingly enough she says yes. But then after you get married, you never talk to her again. Such silence would be evidence of profound ingratitude and a heart grown cold. We talk to those we love.

We also pray because God has ordained means to accomplish His ends. He gives more grace to those who petition Him for it. He grants more of His Spirit to those who long for Him. Sure, God could accomplish His purposes without prayer, but when we pray we are reminded of our dependence on God. If we ask not, we will have not. If we rely on ourselves, God will leave us to ourselves. God doesn't need prayer, but He uses prayer just like He uses other means. He uses rain to grow the crops, sun to warm the earth, and food to strengthen the body. So why can't God choose our prayers to do His sovereign work?

Perhaps the biggest reason why God has us pray (and one reason the Catechism doesn't mention) is for His own glory. God is glorified when He is seen clearly to be the giver of what we asked for in prayer. If we didn't have to ask, we might not notice the answer, and we might forget the one who gave us the blessing. God is glorified in prayer by the expression of our dependence on Him. He is glorified by the faith we put in Him to ask for things. He is glorified when we learn to recognize that every good gift comes down from our Father of lights.

Second, *how* does God want us to pray? The answer is simple: God wants us to pray sincerely, humbly, and confidently. He wants prayer from the heart. Not vain prayer. Not perfunctory prayer. Not pseudospiritual prayer to some nebulous spirit. He wants honest prayer to the one true God. We don't have to come to God pretending to be something we're not. In fact, God doesn't want us to be anything but what we are. Come broken. Come confused. Come hiding nothing and acknowledging everything. Put aside hypocrisy, pretense, and self-reliance and just come. The irony is the more humble our hearts, the more confident we should be. As long as you want to talk to God more than you want to hear from yourself, God will listen to you.

Don't think God can't hear you with all the other millions of people praying to Him. Don't think He won't hear you because of the sin in your past. Christ is your Advocate and He has made a way for you. Pray to God with a sincere heart, a humble spirit, and confidence in Christ's mercy and He will hear your prayers.

Third, *what* does God want us to pray for? In a word: everything. Tell Him about your hurts. Tell Him about your joys. Ask Him where the car keys are. Ask Him for the conversion of your children. Ask Him for health. Ask Him for holiness. He is a loving Father. Ask Him.

Don't get me wrong; God is not a cosmic vending machine. He isn't a jolly St. Nick looking to give us all the toys and presents we want. That's why we must pray for everything *as embraced in the prayer Jesus taught us to pray.* This prayer teaches us what we really need. God wants us to pray for everything we need to hallow His name, everything we need to do His will, everything we need to make it through today, everything we need to flee the Evil One, everything we need to bring Him glory.

Get down deep into the Scripture, God's holy Word, and your prayers will start to fly. We pray best when we ask God for everything He already wants to give us.

120. Q. WHY DID CHRIST COMMAND US TO CALL GOD "OUR FATHER"?

    A. At the very beginning of our prayer Christ wants to kindle in us what is basic to our prayer—the childlike awe and trust that God through Christ has become our Father. Our fathers do not refuse us the things of this life; God our Father will even less refuse to give us what we ask in faith.

121. Q. WHY THE WORDS "IN HEAVEN"?

    A. Those words teach us not to think of God's heavenly majesty as something earthly, and to expect everything for body and soul from His almighty power.

The Indispensable
Fatherhood of God

*C*hrist commands us to call God "our Father." True, God is neither male nor female. He is spirit and doesn't have a body. But He has revealed Himself as Father, not Mother; as King, not Queen; as Husband, not Wife. This doesn't mean the Bible never describes God with maternal characteristics. But it means that if we are to be true to the example of biblical revelation, we ought to pray to God as He has named Himself.

The ancient world was filled with goddesses and heavenly female consorts and in some places a divine feminine principle, so we can't write off masculine language for God as capitulation to culture. Besides, Jesus didn't hesitate to buck the cultural norms (even as it related to women) in other instances, so it would be strange for Him to call God "Father" for fear of upsetting the status quo or being misunderstood. The fact of the matter is, the Son of God related to God as "Father" and commands us to pray to God in such terms. "Our Mother God" is not faithful to Scripture. "Creator, Redeemer, Sanctifier" as a replacement for "Father, Son, and Holy Spirit" is unacceptable.

In short, the unwillingness to acknowledge God as "Father" is an affront to God's gracious and perfect self-disclosure.

Granted, the Fatherhood of God will be challenging for some. Some Christians grew up with weak fathers, abusive fathers, or no father at all. We can sympathize with those for whom "Father" stirs up all sorts of bad connotations. But sympathy does not trump Scripture. We ought to interpret our experiences through God's revelation and not the other way around. So instead of running from the Fatherhood of God because we had a bad father, we ought to let God define true Fatherhood for us and grieve that our fathers fell so far from the divine example. For those who hate their father, learning to love our heavenly Father can bring necessary healing and forgiveness.

Embracing God as Father is part of our discipleship as Christians. We call on God as Father in our prayers to remind us that we are His children and He knows what is best for us. As the Catechism puts it, "childlike awe and trust" are basic to our prayer. I don't know that my kids stand in awe of me. They certainly aren't always obedient. But I can see that they look up to me. They want to do what I do. They copy my actions and mannerisms (for better or worse). They want my attention and approval.

And especially when they are younger, children think their dads are invincible. I don't know about girls, but the boys I knew as a child frequently bantered back and forth, "My dad can beat up your dad" or "My dad is bigger than your dad" or "My dad is smarter than yours." The competition may not have been healthy, but the respect was. Young kids think their dad can do everything. Even when they don't listen to them, kids are in awe of their fathers.

They also trust Dad. My kids (as far as I can tell) never wonder if I'm lacing their oatmeal with arsenic. They don't fear that when I walk them to the park I'm secretly selling them off to Ishmaelite traders. My kids, at least at their young ages, don't doubt that I love them. They grab my hand when crossing the road because it makes them feel safe. There is implicit trust that I will protect them, defend them, and take care of them. This should be our posture in prayer. We are not bowing before a tyrannical despot or distant deity. We are praying to our Father. He's bigger, better, and stronger than any earthly father. He loves us more fiercely, understands us more deeply, and delights in us more fully.

As a dad, I absolutely thrill to see my children happy. I love to help them when they humbly ask for help. I never begrudge feeding them, clothing them, or giving them a bed to sleep in. Even we who are evil know how to give good gifts to our children. How much more, then, does our heavenly Father love to help His brokenhearted children when they come to Him in faith (see Matt. 7:9–11)? Though God may discipline His children and lead us through valleys we would not have chosen, we should never doubt that God is on our side. I am a flawed dad in dozens of ways. But I hope my children will always know that I love them, that I want what is good for them, and will always do what I think is best to help them. All parents wish to do the best for their children, even though our love is weak, our good is not always great, and our help is not always helpful. So how much more ought we who belong to a perfect Father call on Him with complete trust that He loves us, wants what is good for us, and serves us in ways that are best?

What's more, as the Catechism reminds us, *our Father* is in heaven. He is not the smartest guy in town but the all-knowing ruler of the universe. He is not the most influential man on the school board but Lord over all creation.

When we pray to God, we are not petitioning some local power broker or political bigwig or academic know-it-all. We are making our requests before the one who rules over all from His heavenly throne (Q/A 121). As the young theologians sometimes sing, "My God is so big! So strong and so mighty! There's nothing my God cannot do!"

Lord's Day 47

122. Q. WHAT DOES THE FIRST REQUEST MEAN?

A. "Hallowed be Your name" means, Help us to really know You, to bless, worship, and praise You for all Your works and for all that shines forth from them: Your almighty power, wisdom, kindness, justice, mercy, and truth. And it means, help us to direct all our living—what we think, say, and do—so that Your name will never be blasphemed because of us but always honored and praised.

First Things First

The first line of the Lord's Prayer is not a declaration—it's is a request. We are not declaring, "Your name is hallowed." We are petitioning, "May Your name be hallowed!" In other words, Jesus teaches us that the first thing we ought to pray for, before we ask for anything else, is that God would be glorified and set apart as holy.

Few of us have probably stopped to think what radical reorientation flows from this first petition. By putting "hallowed be Your name" first, Jesus would have us understand that the point of prayer is God's glory. Yes, we may legitimately ask for other things, but our overriding concern is for the fame of God's name. It's as if we prayed, "Our Father in heaven, the concern nearest to my heart and the one that shapes all other requests is that Your name would be regarded as holy, that Your fame would be heralded in the earth, that You would be honored among the nations, that Your glory would be magnified for all to see. O Lord, be pleased to cause men everywhere to take pleasure in You, that You might be praised now and forever."

I like the first line in Answer 122: "*Hallowed be Your name* means, Help us to really know You." I sometimes think Christians apologize too much for learning. We are wary of being bigheaded, small-hearted people, and that's a valid concern. But isn't knowing God the goal? Some sermons should not end without three points of "practical" application, because simply knowing God better is the point. Of course, this knowledge is more than mere cognition. But if God is the point, as the first petition of the Lord's Prayer suggests, what could be more important than to grow in our experiential knowledge of Him? No apology is necessary for wanting to know God better.

I need the Lord's Prayer because I need help hallowing God's name.

I do not easily "bless, worship, and praise" God for all His works and all that shines forth from them. It's not that I'm opposed to praise. But my mind is shallow, my discipline weak, and my affections cold. So I pray, "Come Thou fount of every blessing, tune my heart to sing Thy grace." "Hallowed be Your name" prepares our heartstrings to receive the bow of prayer and make a pleasant sound.

When we pray in this way, we not only rightly acknowledge our place in the world—God is the center and we are not—we also align ourselves with God's ultimate purposes. To paraphrase Jonathan Edwards, the chief end for which God created the world is His own glory. In all things, the end design in God's actions and plans is that His name would be glorified. What better way to pray than in alignment with God's chief concern.

"But doesn't this make God into the worst kind of egomaniac?" someone may object. "Isn't this sort of deity just interested in flattery on a cosmic scale?" The answer, of course, is no. Let me give three reasons why.

First, God's passion for His glory is not the same as self-flattery because it does not arise out of weakness or deficiency. Jesus said, "I do not receive glory from people" (John 5:41). Acts 17:24–25 reminds us that "the God who made the world and everything in it, being Lord of heaven and earth, does not live in temples made by man, nor is he served by human hands, *as though he needed anything*, since he himself gives to all mankind life and breath and everything" (italics added). When we hallow God's name, we are not adding to God's intrinsic worth or cheering Him up while others put Him down. God doesn't need our praise as a flatterer needs to be stroked.

Second, we hallow God's name because it deserves to be hallowed. Our objection to self-aggrandizement stems from the fact that extolling our own virtues strikes us as incongruous with our true merit. When we see preening politicians or athletes who can't see past their own glitz and glamor, we are turned off because something inside us says, "Nobody is that important. You are not as wonderful as you'd like us to think you are." But things are different with God. To recognize that God is the most glorious, most lovely, most powerful Being in the universe is to simply recognize Him for who He is. To boast in the highest point in Iowa as a lofty peak is ridiculous, but to hail Mount Everest as the tallest mountain on the planet is justice.

Third, hallowing God's name is for our good. God's glory and God's love are not at odds. God's desire to be glorified is not opposed to His desire for our joy. Parents want their kids to put their hopes in something solid. We don't want them to think happiness comes ultimately from playing football or going to Yale or getting hammered every weekend. We want their desires to terminate on something that will satisfy. God has the same desire for His children. He wants us to have lasting joy, which is why He directs our attention to His glory. As John Piper says, God is most glorified in us when we are most satisfied in Him. Or to put it another way, our greatest good is to rejoice in God's great glory.

When we pray "Our Father in heaven, hallowed be Your name," we are not only asking for God's fame to spread, among the nations and in our hearts, we are also asking implicitly for our lasting joy. "Not to us, O Lord, not to us, but your name give glory" (Ps. 115:1) is the prayer of a wise and happy man.

122. Q. WHAT DOES THE SECOND REQUEST MEAN?

A. "Your kingdom come" means, Rule us by Your Word and Spirit in such a way that more and more we submit to You. Keep Your church strong, and add to it. Destroy the devil's work; destroy every force which revolts against You and every conspiracy against Your Word. Do this until Your kingdom is so complete and perfect that in it You are all in all.

The Kingdom and the King

*I*n commenting on "Your kingdom come," the second request of the Lord's Prayer, John Calvin begins with an unusual claim: "This contains nothing new . . ."[54] Strange as it sounds, Calvin is right. Once we've prayed for God's name to be hallowed, have we not also prayed for His kingdom to come (and His will to be done, for that matter)? Where God's name is set apart as holy, His commands will be obeyed and His reign will be acknowledged.

"Rule us by Your Word and Spirit in such a way that more and more we submit to You," is how the Catechism puts it. In other words, the kingdom has come where the King has His way. Faith and repentance, and the godly life that follows in their wake, are unchangeable requirements for membership in the kingdom. We want to live like Christ, show people Christ, and make a difference for Christ, but also call people to renounce their rebellion against God, flee worldliness, and be ready to meet the King when He returns to finally establish His kingdom in full. God is not interested in making us good people apart from making us glory people. That is to say, the kingdom is not about excellence in behavior. It's about our willing submission to God and living a life of love that befits those who belong to such a lovely King.

There is a strong connection, which the Catechism picks up on, between the kingdom and the church, which is why the Catechism says the two should not be separated, as if we can ignore the church to focus on the kingdom. There is nothing more important in all the world for the fulfillment of God's plans and the spread of His glory than strong churches.

And yet, there are so many ways the church is weak. It is often doctrinally compromised and theologically uninformed. It suffers at times from poor planning, paltry vision, and lack of follow-through. It can be love-less, listless, and indifferent to the needs of others. The church is torn apart by schism, heresies, and persecution. Too often, it is in desperate need of godly leadership and faithful preaching. Some churches are all style and no substance. Other churches are ready to close their doors for want of money and members. There are legalistic churches, shallow churches, mean churches, lazy churches, and worldly churches. Amidst so much weakness, every Christian should plead with God, "Keep Your church strong."

"And add to it." We should pray for conversions too. Yes, the Reformed care about the lost too. Granted, the Heidelberg Catechism does not have a well-developed doctrine of missions or evangelism, but in texts like this we get glimpses of the Reformation heart for conversion. As the old hymn says, "We long to see Your churches full, that all the chosen race, may with one voice and heart and soul, sing Your redeeming grace."

It bears mentioning at this point that the kingdom and the church are not identical. The relationship between the two is complex. If the Reformers, steeped as they were in Christendom, tended to equate the two, self-proclaimed reformers in our day tend to separate the two as if the church could be forgotten in our attempts to build the kingdom. George Ladd, the preeminent evangelical scholar on the kingdom in the last fifty years, saw five different aspects in the relationship between the kingdom and the church: (1) the church is not the kingdom; (2) the kingdom creates the church; (3) the church gives witness to the kingdom; (4) the church acts as the instrument of the kingdom; and (5) the church acts as custodian of the kingdom.[55] This means that the coming kingdom (God's increasing reign and rule) is not confined to the church but the citizens of the kingdom are. It also means that our prayer for the kingdom to come is not only a prayer for the strength of the church but for the spread of righteousness, justice, grace, and submission to God's Word in the world.

Having considered the church's place in the kingdom, the Catechism then turns to the opponents of the kingdom. If the kingdom of God is where our King reigns and rules, where His enemies are put in subjection under His feet, then in praying for the kingdom to come, we must pray for the conquering of the King's enemies. We are not praying a namby-pamby prayer for niceness to take over the world. We are asking God to crush His enemies, vanquish His foes, and destroy every power that rises in opposition to His Christ and His Word. As Calvin puts it, "God sets up His kingdom by humbling the world."[56]

The concluding line—"Do this until Your kingdom is so complete and perfect that in it You are all"—can guard us from serious error. Theologians like to talk of the "already and the not yet" of the kingdom. That is, the kingdom has been inaugurated, but it has not been fully established. So Jesus can announce the kingdom of God is in the midst of you (Luke 17:21) and also instruct us to pray that the kingdom would come (Matt. 6:10). It has arrived and is still arriving. This means, on the one hand, we should not think of the kingdom of God as Christ's millennial reign sometime in the future. And on the other hand, we should not expect the kingdom to exist among us now in a utopian world of peace and brotherly love. An "already and not yet" understanding of the kingdom gives us hope for improvement in the world, tempered by a realism that acknowledges the continuing presence of sin, enmity, and rebellion.

Lord's Day 49

122. Q. WHAT DOES THE THIRD REQUEST MEAN?

A. "Your will be done on earth as it is in heaven" means, Help us and all people to reject our own wills and to obey Your will without any back talk. Your will alone is good. Help us one and all to carry out the work we are called to, as willingly and faithfully as the angels in heaven.

Willing and Walking

few phrases are more confusing to the Christian than "the will of God."[57] The confusion is partly owing to the variety of uses in the Bible. On the one hand, God works all things according to the counsel of His will (Eph. 1:11). God's will, in this sense, cannot be overturned, negated, or thwarted. What God wills will come to pass. But on the other hand, we must pray for God's will to be done. The fact that we must pray for His will to be done on earth as it is in heaven implies that the will of God, in this sense, can be disobeyed and ignored.

We can think of these two sides of God's will as His will of decree and His will of desire. In the mystery of divine sovereignty and human responsibility, God superintends His creation down to the fine details of hairs and sparrows, and yet His commands can be disregarded by His rebellious creatures.

The Lord's Prayer is concerned with God's will of desire. In heaven the angels always do God's bidding and the saints ever live to sing His praises. There is perfect holiness, perfect obedience, and perfect worship. Jesus commands us, therefore, to pray that God's will be done on earth just as it is in heaven.

According to the Catechism, this request from the Lord's Prayer entails three things. *First, we reject our own wills.* The longer I'm a pastor, the more I see that this is the real battle going on in the hearts of men, women, and children. Many times people come to me with a pressing burden or struggle, and on several of those occasions, it quickly becomes clear this person or couple came to see their pastor in hopes that he would affirm them in doing what they were feeling was not right. It's as if they had already decided what they wanted to do and had a sense that it would be frowned upon by the church, and even God's

Word, yet they were looking for some sort of permission or acceptance of their rationale. The struggle, at the most basic heart level, was whether to follow their will or God's.

That's the whole difficulty with being a Christian. God gets to make the rules, and we don't like it.

It takes faith to die to ourselves. We will not reject our own wills unless we believe that God's will is better.

Which brings us to the *second point: We must trust God's will.* "Your will alone is good," Answer 122 tells us. To pray the Lord's Prayer takes a lot of believing guts. Our whole system of American government is designed so that no one alone can have their will be done all the time. The framers of the Constitution figured no one can be trusted with that kind of power. They were right. Would you dare to tell your husband at the start of each day, "Honey, your will be done"? Even if he's a swell guy, no one deserves to have his will followed no matter what. No one except for God. When we pray "Your will be done," we are confessing our confidence that God knows best, that His plans are good, that His way is always the right way.

If we are to be faithful and sincere in our prayers, we will have to learn to steadfastly love the will of God as David did. In Psalm 119 he wrote, "Your testimonies are wonderful; therefore my soul keeps them. The unfolding of your words gives light; it imparts understanding to the simple. I open my mouth and pant, because I long for your commandments. . . . Make your face shine upon your servant, and teach me your statutes. My eyes shed streams of tears, because people do not keep your law" (vv. 129–31, 135–36).

Don't let these words pass by too quickly. We are too prone to read spiritual words as constant hyperbole. But pay attention to David's language. He longed for God's commands and pleaded with God to know them because they were wonderful and gave light. On the flip side, he balled his eyes out to see so much disobedience in the land. Who will weep for needless divorces, aborted babies, rebellious teens, selfish fathers, and spiteful mothers? Who will put away the pounding fist, the cowardly tolerance, and the cynic's laugh and instead shed streams of tears because sexual deviants, greedy loan sharks, duplicitous politicians, phony Christians, and prideful pastors do not keep the law of God? The will of God alone is good and we distrust it to our shame and our hurt.

Third, we must carry out God's will. It does us no good, nor anyone else, if we love the will of God and long for it to be accomplished, but never carry it out ourselves. Here especially is where we must rely on prayer because the old Kevin (or the old Karen) is neither willing nor able to carry out God's commands.

That's why we pray, "Open my eyes, that I may behold wondrous things out of your law" (Ps. 119:18). And, "Turn my eyes from looking at worthless things" (v. 37). We need divine help so that God's will becomes our will. Then we can say, "Your testimonies are my delight" (v. 24). And, "I love your commandments above gold, above fine gold. . . . I hate every false way" (vv. 127–28).

God must make us willing. And God alone can make us able. "Keep me steady according to your promise, and let no iniquity get dominion over me" is the cry of every true Christian (v. 133). The will of God is not our duty or drudgery. It is our delight.

And yet, it is a tortuous delight. It requires struggle against sin and the fight of faith. It means death, death, and more death. It would seem easier for God to simply annihilate our wills and infuse our souls with His. But that's not His way. He prefers slow, glorious growth. He doesn't want His will in us as much as He wants our will to be His. He wants us to want what He wants, love what He loves, and hate what He hates.

Better keep praying.

125. Q. WHAT DOES THE FOURTH REQUEST MEAN?

A. "Give us today our daily bread" means, Do take care of all our physical needs so that we come to know that You are the only source of everything good, and that neither our work and worry nor Your gifts can do us any good without Your blessings. And so help us to give up our trust in creatures and to put trust in You alone.

Prayerlessness Is Unbelief

$\mathcal{G}$ ive us this day our daily bread." I can't decide if this is the request we pray the most or pray the least. On the one hand, it seems that we pray this prayer more than any other. It's easy for us to think of our needs (and wants!) and ask God to give us things. But on the other hand, how often do we really pray for our daily bread? Sure, we pray when tragedies strike or peculiar difficulties show us our need of God. But day after day, we neglect this most basic request.

For example, almost all of us assume there will be food on the table. We assume we will be taken care of. For most of our lives, we even assume we will be healthy. We see the need to pray for the kingdom, for our need for forgiveness, even on behalf of God's name being hallowed. But we simply don't think our daily bread demands our daily attention.

Our gratitude to God for His daily provision should be passionate and frequent because His grace to us has been so mind-boggling. Living in America, we are the recipients of so much common grace. Because of advances in agriculture and technology, we do not worry about the lack of rain in July. Sure, the farmers worry what it will do to their crops, but families don't seriously worry that a dry summer will mean starvation for us in the winter (though we may fret over higher prices at the store). We have grocery stores filled with food all year long. All we have to do is take an hour and go fill up our carts. The hardest parts of getting our daily bread are the choices we must make among so many options and the pounds we must shed afterward.

Granted, even in America there are millions who go hungry and plenty of families who do worry about next week's groceries. I'm not suggesting we have food issues taken care of in this country. But our lack is to a far lesser degree than that in other parts of the world. For a myriad of reasons, hunger and malnutrition continue to be among the most pressing problems on the planet. All the more reason we have to give abundant thanks to God for giving almost all of us our daily bread day after ungrateful day.

I'm struck by the line in the Catechism that our work, our worry, and our gifts cannot do any good without God's blessing. The great danger we have, living in such an affluent society, is the evil of self-reliance. How tempted we are to think that we are in control, that we are gifted enough, hardworking enough, and rich enough to tackle any problem. But the reality is God can frustrate the best laid plans of mice and Americans. Unless the Lord builds the house, those who build it labor in vain (Ps. 127:1).

This is why prayer is so essential for the Christian. The simple act of getting on our knees (or faces or feet or whatever) for five or fifty minutes every day is the surest sign of our humility and dependence on God. There may be many reasons for our prayerlessness—time management, busyness, lack of concentration—but most fundamentally, we ask not because we think we need not. Deep down we feel secure when we have money in the bank, a healthy report from the doctor, and powerful people on our side. We do not trust in God alone. Prayerlessness is an expression of our meager confidence in God's ability to provide and of our strong confidence in our ability to take care of ourselves without God's help.

Too often when we struggle with prayer we focus on the wrong things. We focus on praying better instead of focusing on knowing better the one to whom we pray. And we focus on our need for discipline rather than our need for God. So many of us want to pray more but our lives seem too disordered. But God wants us to see that our messy, chaotic lives can be an impetus to prayer instead of an obstacle to prayer.

You don't need discipline nearly as much as you need a broken heart and faith. You don't need an ordered life to enable prayer, you need a messy life to drive you to prayer. You don't need to have everything together to pray. You need to know you're not together so you will pray. You don't need your life to be fixed up before you pray. You need a broken heart. You need to realize "Tomorrow is another day that I need God. I need to know Him. I need forgiveness. I need help. I need protection. I need deliverance. I need patience. I need courage." And because of all those needs, you realize you need prayer. If you know you are needy and believe that God helps the needy, you will pray.

If we never pray, the problem goes much deeper than a lack of organization and follow-through. The heart that never talks to God is the heart that trusts in itself and not in the power of God. Prayerlessness is unbelief. And the opposite of this attitude? "Give us this day our daily bread."

*L*ord's Day 51

126. Q. WHAT DOES THE FIFTH REQUEST MEAN?

A. "Forgive us our debts, as we also have forgiven our debtors" means,
Because of Christ's blood, do not hold against us, poor sinners
that we are, any of the sins we do or the evil that constantly clings
to us. Forgive us just as we are fully determined, as evidence of
Your grace in us, to forgive our neighbors.

Getting It and
Giving It Away

We need daily bread that we might live. We need daily forgiveness that we might not die. How have we fallen short of the glory of God? Let us count the ways.

With little sleep and pressing responsibilities, you fire a harsh word at your children, "Stop it! You're driving me crazy!" Feeling hurt by your wife, you let loose a biting remark, "You'd hate to be helpful, wouldn't you?" Wanting your body to be your own instead of your husband's, you pretend to have a headache rather than follow through on your promise of a romantic evening. Imagining yourself all-important and all-knowing, you pout at your parents for setting boundaries in your life.

The apostle James is right: We all stumble in many ways (James 3:2). We need forgiveness every day because we rack up debts every day. On our best days, our perfect God gets only imperfect obedience and imperfect worship from us. We are hopeless debtors.

"But," you may ask, "I thought when I repented of my sins and asked Jesus into my heart, my sins were forgiven and I was declared right with God, so why do I need to ask for forgiveness? Aren't all my sins—past, present, and future—already taken care of in Christ?"

The answer to that last question is yes and no. In a legal sense, all my sins were nailed to the cross. My sin was imputed to Christ while Christ's righteousness was reckoned to me. That's what it means to be justified. I stand before God the judge and He declares, "You, Kevin DeYoung, miserable sinner, are innocent and pure because you are in Christ." In a legal sense, I am declared righteous.

In a relational sense, however, I must continually seek restoration and forgiveness. Even though I am in Christ, I still say, do, and think things that are foul, corrupt, and offensive to God. This is the point of 1 John 1:8–9, which is really just a commentary on the sin offering of Leviticus 4 and 5. If we say we are without sin, we lie and "the truth is not in us. But if we confess our sins, [God] is faithful and just to forgive us our sins and to cleanse us from all unrighteousness."

So if I sin as a Christian, I should not fear condemnation—for there is no condemnation for those who are in Christ Jesus (Rom. 8:1)—but if my conscience is working as it should, I will still feel guilty. Sin is still displeasing to God. Imagine your son has a paper route. You tell your son, "You must do the paper route. It's your job, not mine." But one day he purposely skips the route to play with his friends after school. You happen to notice a lonely stack of papers waiting to be delivered. So you load up your car and deliver the papers for him. When he gets home, you want to talk with the boy. Now, you're not going to disown him, but he's been disobedient so there is a strain in the relationship. The parent-child relationship has been disturbed by the son's disobedience.

But if your son comes sorrowfully, "I blew it, Dad [or Mom]. I promised you wouldn't ever have to do my route and I broke that promise. I'm sorry. Forgive me." Now the relationship is restored. If the son were to carry on with habitual disobedience without asking for forgiveness, the relationship would grow more and more distant. That's why we must continually come to God for forgiveness, with similar language: "I blew it. I broke my promise. I am guilty before You. Please forgive me." A broken heart and contrite spirit God will never deny.

But, of course, the Lord's Prayer doesn't stop with "Forgive us our debts." We also pray "As we forgive our debtors." That begs the question, What exactly is forgiveness? The context of the Lord's Prayer helps us formulate a definition. Forgiveness involves canceling a debt or remitting a payment. Forgiveness doesn't mean the consequences of our actions will always be removed (e.g., the thief on the cross didn't get to live just because he was forgiven), nor does it mean we can't be discerning in our judgments about others. Forgiveness is not a feeling but a decision to let go of the debt owed us. Forgiveness means we say no to revenge, trusting that God is the one to avenge (Rom. 12:17–21). Forgiveness means our sins are no longer counted against us and we no longer count the sins of those who have hurt us.

In one sense, we should forgive all those who sin against us. We should not seek their harm. We should pray for them and desire their good. But in another sense, forgiveness can be granted only to those who seek it. That is, while we should always be ready to forgive, unless the other party is willing to repent, forgiveness cannot reach its full bloom. Forgiveness implies the restoration of a relationship, and without repentance a broken relationship cannot truly be restored.

So hear without reservation the Bible's demand that we forgive as we have been forgiven. As long as there is repentance, there must be forgiveness (Matt. 18:21–22). "For if you forgive others their trespasses, your heavenly Father will also forgive you, but if you do not forgive others their trespasses, neither will your Father forgive your trespasses" (Matt. 6:14–15). The unforgiving heart is the unforgiven heart.

Does this mean unforgiving people then lose their salvation? No. Rather, a black, stony unforgiving heart is evidence of a heart that has never truly experienced God's forgiveness. If my mortgage company calls me up tomorrow and tells me my mortgage is canceled, and then Sallie Mae calls and tells me my student loans are remitted, and I really believe this good news—know it, taste it, experience it—will I berate my friend after supper when he sticks me with the tip? Not a chance. I've known too much grace to be so graceless (see Matt. 18:23–35).

You and I deserved hell. We were hopeless, helpless, and heavenless. But now we have life, redemption, forgiveness, and glory. If our lives are still marked by bitterness, grudges, and thoughts of retribution, we just don't get it. You haven't understood forgiveness until you've given it away.

Lord's Day 52

127. Q. WHAT DOES THE SIXTH REQUEST MEAN?

A. "And lead us not into temptation, but deliver us from the evil one" means, By ourselves we are too weak to hold our own even for a moment. And our sworn enemies—the devil, the world, and our own flesh—never stop attacking us. And so, Lord, uphold us and make us strong with the strength of Your Holy Spirit, so that we may not go down to defeat in this spiritual struggle, but may firmly resist our enemies until we finally win the complete victory.

128. Q. WHAT DOES YOUR CONCLUSION TO THIS PRAYER MEAN?

A. "For Yours is the kingdom and the power and the glory forever" means, We have made all these requests of You because, as our all-powerful King, You not only want to, but are able to give us all that is good; and because Your holy name, and not we ourselves, should receive all the praise, forever.

129. Q. WHAT DOES THAT LITTLE WORD "AMEN" EXPRESS?

A. "Amen" means, This is sure to be! It is even more sure that God listens to my prayer, than that I really desire what I pray for.

"This Is Sure to Be!"

*J*esus taught His disciples a number of things about prayer. But the most consistent lesson He taught them was also the simplest: pray. We might wish that Jesus gave more forms for prayer, like the Lord's Prayer we've been studying, or that He did more to explain prayer and God's sovereignty or that He gave us more insights on how to become disciplined in our prayer times. But the main thing He wanted to convey was simply to pray. "Come to Me. Talk to Me. Ask me. Just ask Me."

Yes, there are wrong ways to pray, but the most important part of prayer is actually praying. God loves it when we pray, because sincere, honest prayer in Jesus' name shows two of the most essential virtues in a Christian: humility and trust. When we ask God for help, we are saying, "God, I cannot figure this out. I can't do it on my own. But You can help. You can change things. You can rescue me." Mature Christian prayer always glorifies God because it is always humble and always confident. It believes the battle is not ours but God's (2 Chron. 20:15).

The sixth petition of the Lord's Prayer reminds us that life is a spiritual struggle. It is the measure of our carelessness that we pray the sixth request so infrequently. (In fact, it's not a bad idea to pray the Lord's Prayer every day. At the very least, it would be good for our spiritual lives to often make the substance of these requests our personal requests.) Too many of us face the day giving little thought to our enemies. If we were in a physical war, we would scout out our enemies' positions each morning and plan carefully for possible attacks and counterattacks. But when it comes to spiritual battle, we suffer from gross overconfidence. Our sworn enemies—the flesh, the world, and the Devil—are not at rest, so neither should we be. This very day we will face temptations to cave to peer pressure, temptations to follow that alluring link on the Internet, temptations to bad-mouth our parents, temptations to make shipwreck of the faith. How earnestly we ought to pray for protection against our thoughts, the world's lies, and the Devil's stratagems.

There is no cruise control for Christianity. Each day is a fight. Daily we must look for the Lord's mercy that we might keep ourselves in the love of God (Jude 21).

The reason we pray with such vigor is for our own survival and for the glory of the Lord. I often think of what a disaster for the Lord's glory I could become. I don't think this with morbid fear, but with a healthy sense of my own sinfulness and my desperate need for God's daily grace. I want my life to make God look precious, powerful, and pure, not weak, duplicitous, and insignificant. This is where the conclusion to the Lord's Prayer is so helpful. Granted, the last line of the Lord's Prayer, because of poor manuscript evidence, is not found in newer English translations. But we can still say the line with confidence, knowing it is an allusion to David's prayer in 1 Chronicles 29:11. The end of the Lord's Prayer reminds us that God is an all-powerful King able to help us, an all-glorious King who deservers our praise forever.

The last Question and Answer is beautifully simple. The Catechism explains that "Amen" is not short for "prayer over" but means "Truly!" "Verily!" or "This is sure to be!" I knew a guy in college who, in an act of quasi-rebellion, decided to end all his prayers with "Groovy" instead of "Amen." It never ceased to annoy me. Thankfully most people found "Groovy" lacking the necessary gravitas, so the world hasn't switched over yet. Even more importantly, I love what the Catechism says about the promise we have in "Amen": "It is even more sure that God listens to my prayer, than that I really desire what I pray for." Think of that next time you "Amen" your prayer. God is so gracious that He is more willing to hear our requests than we are sure that we actually want what we pray for.

How liberating! Go ahead and pray to God better than you feel and you may just find that in His mercy you end up better than you deserve.

Epilogue:
The Crust and the Core

This has been a book about theology, about knowing theology and loving theology. But if we've really paid attention to the Heidelberg Catechism, this should also be a book about warmhearted experiential faith. In fact, knowing and loving theological truth is what produces the warmhearted experiential faith.

Sadly, too many Christians are asked to choose between theology and experience, between head and heart, between having convictions and being kind. These are false dichotomies—choices that don't have to be made. We are to love the Lord Jesus with *every* part of us—all our heart, all our soul, all our strength, and all our mind too (Luke 10:27). We ought to be hugging theologians—people marked by abiding grace and unchanging truth. Or to put it another way, if we are to be fruitful and godly Christians, we need to have a theological core without being theologically crusty.

In desiring a theological core, I don't mean that all Christians must be bookish and given to intellectual contemplation. I mean that every Christian must be shaped from the inside out by a set of convictions about who God is and what He has accomplished in Jesus Christ. As Christians we should be animated (given life) and motivated (compelled to action) by a core of doctrinal truths—truths such as: (1) God is loving, sovereign, and holy; (2) God created the world and created it good; (3) as a result of Adam's sin humans are bent toward evil; (4) Jesus Christ is God's Son, begotten not created; (5) Jesus suffered and died on the cross for sins and rose again on the third day; (6) the Holy

Spirit is God and fills us with power, enables us to believe, equips us with gifts, and bears fruit in our lives. Add to those core truths these three: The Bible is God's Word; Jesus is coming again to judge the living and the dead; and justification is by faith alone.

These truths need to be more than a set of beliefs we assume. They should be the lens through which we look at ourselves and the world. There are many Christians and churches that don't deny any cardinal doctrine of Christian faith, but they still don't have a theological core. They have, instead, a musty statement of faith they barely understand and hardly believe and wouldn't dare preach. They are animated and motivated by politics, church growth, relational concerns, and the like, but the gospel is merely assumed. "Yes, yes, of course we believe in the virgin birth, the atonement, the resurrection, and heaven and hell," they say. But it's all periphery, not core. It's all assumed, not all-consuming.

Theologically hollow congregations and pastors may like to think they will bequeath a gospel legacy to the next generation, but the truth is we only pass on what is our passion. New converts and new kids won't think and live and love like mature Christians, let alone be able to articulate the Christian story, if our beliefs rest in a pamphlet and not in our hearts.

I make no apologies for my church being a theological church. The church ought to be about the business of the gospel, and the gospel is a message of historical fact plus God-given interpretation. That's theology. I hope we never feel like we have the "theology thing" down at our church just because we have solid book studies and long, meaty sermons. The "theology thing" is a lifelong project of being transformed by the renewing of our minds. We want to be thinking Christians who know what we believe, why we believe it, and live and die in the comfort of these beliefs.

Having a theological core means, among other things, that our unity is theological. Of course we want to be united in love and purpose too. But whatever actions and affections we share in unison ought to radiate from a theological core. There is so much talk around the broader church about being missional Christians that it's easy to think the church should be missional-centric. And in one sense, mission is certainly at the center of what we do. But mission itself is not what should tie us together. It's only when the mission is defined and its genesis is proclaimed that we can rally around mission.

What I mean is that we should be, first of all, Christocentric, that is, centered on the cross of Christ. Christ is our identity, our passion, and our hope. And because of this identity, passion, and hope, we pray and evangelize and do missions. But missions is not the center. Christ is—this shapes, defines, and launches us into mission. It's like John Piper's famous line: "Mission is not the ultimate goal of the church. Worship is." Being *missional* is not a sufficient basis for unity. One, because we're never quite sure what *missional* means. Two, because the blazing hot center of Christian identity, passion, and hope is not that we are all doing things in Jesus' name. Of course, we should be doing things in Jesus' name. Instead, the blazing hot center is what God has already done for us in Christ. This must always be explained and rejoiced in, not merely assumed.

Which brings me back to the main point. We desperately need Christians and pastors and missionaries and churches and denominations and movements and institutions that are theological to the core, where doctrines are not simply items to be checked off the dogmatic grocery list nor statements to be dusted off out of the ecclesiastical attic. We must all be theological because being a Christian means we embrace a message about who Jesus is and the victory He won for us. And that's theology.

So, core, yes. Crust? No.

Please, don't skip this last part, especially if you really liked the first part. Because you may just be a crusty Christian if you're not careful.

What makes a Christian crusty? A number of things. For starters, it's an attitude. It's a demeanor where being Calvinist or paedobaptist or inerrantist (three things I am gladly) are put on like armor or wielded like weapons, when they are meant to be the warm glow of a Christian whose core radiates with love for Christ and the gospel. I believe in theological distinctives—I believe in them and I believe it is good to have them—but if the distinctives are not manifestly the flower of gospel root, the buds aren't worth the blooming.

A second mark of crusty Christians is approachability, as in, not having any. There is a sizing up-ness that makes some theological types unnecessarily prickly. They are bright and opinionated and quickly analytical. They can also be incessantly critical. Crusty Christians are hard to be around. They are intimidating instead of engaging and growling instead

244 THE GOOD NEWS WE ALMOST FORGOT

of gracious. They are too willing to share their opinions on everything and unable to put any doctrine in any category not marked "absolutely essential."

When theology is more crust than core, it's not so much that we care about good theology too much, we just don't care about some other hugely important things in the same proportion. So we end up largely skeptical of a prayerful, fruitful, warmhearted, godly, Arminian leaning pastor. Now, I might think such a pastor is prayerful, fruitful, warmhearted, and godly despite too much emphasis on libertarian free will, but I sure hope to be mighty thankful for all his prayerfulness, fruitfulness, and warm-hearted godliness. Some Christians allow evangelism to trump all other considerations; others size up fellow Christians by their attention to social justice concerns; but a lot of us do our judging with theology. If the theology fits, the lack of mission, prayer, and compassion doesn't matter much. But if a few theological pieces are misplaced in the puzzle, see you later and don't let Hymenaeus and Philetus's door hit you on the way out (1 Tim. 1:19–20; 2 Tim. 2:16–18).

Striking the balance is not easy. But let's try hard to be discerning and grounded without always looking for the next theological misstep in our friends, our family, or the songs we sing. And let's be able to tell the difference between wandering sheep and false teachers. We must delineate between a slightly ill-informed wording of a phrase and a purposeful rejection of truth. We must pursue a passion for fidelity to Scripture and a winsomeness that sweetens the already honeylike drippings of the Word of God. Let us be more like a chocolate-covered raisin, likeable on the outside and surprisingly good for you on the inside, and less like a Tootsie Pop with its brittle, crunchy exterior that must be broken through before anyone can get to the good stuff.

If it is worth anything, our theological heart will pulse throughout our spiritual bodies, making us into people who are more prayerful, more godly, and more passionate about the Bible, the lost, and the world around us. We will be theologically solid to the core, without the unnecessary crust. Kind of like the Heidelberg Catechism. And kind of like Jesus too.

Appendix:
Does the Heidelberg Catechism Forbid Homosexual Behavior?

For most Christians, the issue of homosexuality does not need to be settled by some sixteenth-century catechism. Texts from Romans 1, 1 Corinthians 6, 1 Timothy 1, Leviticus 18 and 20, and Jude make clear what every first-century Jew would have perfectly understood: Same-sex acts are a violation of the Seventh Commandment and offensive in God's eyes. But since the sinfulness of homosexuality is, sadly, a controversial topic in the Reformed Church in America (and other denominations like mine), whether or not our confessions address the issue becomes an important question.

An investigation of the authorial intent behind Q/A 87 leads us to the conclusion that, almost certainly, the Catechism means to forbid homosexual behavior. Interestingly enough, but not at all surprising, the Presbyterian Church (USA) recently voted to change the wording of Q/A 87 to remove a previous reference to homosexuality in their translation of the Catechism. The 1962 translation of the Catechism by Allen Miller and Eugene Osterhaven (longtime professor at Western Theological Seminary) includes "homosexual perversion" in the list of sins mentioned in Answer 87. The New Christian Reformed Church translation employed in these pages uses the word "unchaste." The difference lays with the fact that Osterhaven and Miller, recognizing correctly that Answer 87 is a paraphrase of 1 Corinthians 6:9–10, included the full Corinthians text from the New English Bible in their translation. Admittedly, this is poor translation practice, which is why the CRC translation simply translates the German word *unkeuscher* with "unchaste." The newer translation is better. But Osterhaven and Miller were at least—and this is according to their own stated purpose—trying to capture the authorial intent behind the text. The translation is poor, but they were right about the meaning.

In summarizing 1 Corinthians 6:9–10, Ursinus (Heidelberg's chief author) does not include every sin in the vice list. Most notably, he leaves out several terms related to sexual immorality. This is certainly not because Ursinus and the Reformers were ambiguous in their assessment of homosexuality. The reason no explicit mention is made of homosexuality in Answer 87 is because it was considered inappropriate and obscene to even mention such deeds in the sixteeenth century. That's why the Catechism includes the phrase "or the like"—we are meant to fill in the blanks with the rest of the text, the part of the text not fit to be printed for all to see.

As Robert Gagnon, probably the world's foremost scholar on homosexuality and the Bible, points out, when Calvin comments on Romans 1:26–27; 1 Corinthians 6:9; and Jude 7 in his commentaries he mentions homosexuality only obliquely, referring to the actions and desires as "monstrous," "polluted," "most filthy and detestable," and "the most abominable." Gagnon also notes that as late as the early twentieth century, the standard edition of ancient Greek texts (Loeb Classical Library, Harvard Univ. Press) "would routinely render Greek classical texts into Latin rather than English whenever coming across favorable discussions of homosexual practice."[58] To talk or write openly about homosexuality was, for many, simply impolite.

Furthermore, we must remember that Frederick's first purpose in commissioning the Heidelberg Catechism was "that our youth may be trained." The Catechism was meant first of all for children, and children, it was thought, should not be corrupted by exposure to such unnatural behavior. Adults would have understood that Answer 87 forbids all the vices mentioned in 1 Corinthians 6:9–10, including the ones left out or too unseemly to mention.

Clearly, Ursinus believed homosexual behavior to be a sin. In his commentary on the Catechism, he defined marriage as "a lawful and indissoluble union between one man and one woman, instituted by God for the propagation of the human race . . ."[59] Just as importantly, he said with regard to the Seventh Commandment: "The first class or kind [of lust] are those which are contrary to nature, and from the devil—such as are even contrary to this our corrupt nature; not only because they are corrupt and spoil it of conformity with God, but also because this our corrupt nature shrinks from them and abhors them. The lusts of which the Apostle Paul speaks in the first chapter of his Epistle to the Romans, are of this class, as the confounding of the sexes, also abuses of the female sex."[60] Not only do we see here an unmistakable rejection of homosexual behavior, we also see Ursinus's reticence to talk of it in frank terms, referring to such behavior as "the confounding of the sexes" and "the lusts of which the Apostle Paul speaks in the first chapter of his Epistle to the Romans."

There is incontrovertible evidence, then, that the chief author of the Heidelberg Catechism thought homosexuality a sin (which should come as no surprise because everyone thought it was a sin in the sixteenth century). We also have good evidence that Christians of the sixteenth century, not to mention Ursinus himself, were embarrassed to name openly the act of same-sex intercourse. We also have evidence in the words "or the like" that we are meant to mentally fill in the blanks with the rest of 1 Corinthians 6:9–10 referenced in Answer 87.

All of this leads to the strong conclusion that while Osterhaven and Miller may have been wrong, from the standpoint of translation philosophy, to insert words in the Catechism that weren't there in the original, they were not wrong to think that the words they inserted, including "homosexual perversion," captured the spirit of the Catechism and the true authorial intent of the text, not to mention the clear teaching of Scripture.

Notes

1. For more on the history of the Catechism, see Lyle D. Bierma et al., *An Introduction to the Heidelberg Catechism: Sources, History, and Theology* (Grand Rapids: Baker, 2005). For general information on the history, theology, practice, and continuing relevance of the Heidelberg Catechism, see *The Church's Book of Comfort*, ed. Willem Van't Spijker, trans. Gerrit Bilkes (Grand Rapids: Reformation Heritage Books, 2009).

2. *Reformed Confessions Harmonized with an Annotated Bibliography of Reformed Doctrinal Works*, ed. Joel R. Beeke and Sinclair B. Ferguson (Grand Rapids: Baker, 1999), x.

3. This metaphor comes from G. I. Williamson, *The Heidelberg Catechism: A Study Guide* (Phillipsburg, N.J.: Presbyterian and Reformed, 1993). Other commentaries include: Fred H. Klooster, *Our Only Comfort: A Comprehensive Commentary on the Heidelberg Catechism, Volumes One and Two* (Grand Rapids: Faith Alive, 2001) and *The Commentary of Dr. Zacharias Ursinus of the Heidelberg Catechism*, trans. G. W. Willard (Phillipsburg, N.J.: Presbyterian and Reformed, 1852 [reprint]).

4. The edition of the Heidelberg Catechism used throughout this book is reprinted from *Ecumenical Creeds and Reformed Confessions* (Grand Rapids: Faith Alive Christian Resources, 1988). Pronouns of the deity in the Catechism have been capitalized throughout to conform to the style of the publisher.

5. John Calvin, *Institutes of the Christian Religion*, III, vii.1, ed. John T. McNeil, trans. Ford Lewis Battles (Philadelphia: Westminster Press, 1960),   .

6. *The Commentary of Dr. Zacharias Ursinus on the Heidelberg Catechism*, trans. G. W. Williard (1852; repr., Phillipsburg, N. J.: Presbyterian and Reformed Publishing, 1985), 17–18.

7. Leon Morris, *The Apostolic Preaching of the Cross* (Grand Rapids: Eerdmans, 1984), 144–213.

8. The thoughts and some of the phrasing of this paragraph come from John Stott, *The Cross of Christ* (Downer's Grove, Ill.: InterVarsity, 2006), 158–59.

9. Quoted in Robert Letham. *The Holy Trinity* (Phillipsburg, N.J.: Presbyterian and Reformed Publishing, 2004), 2.

10. Ibid., 1.

11. Ibid.

12. Robert L. Millet, *A Different Jesus* (Grand Rapids: Eerdmans, 2005), 70, 141.

13. My thinking on these three points is influenced by Letham, *The Holy Trinity*, 7–13, 407–78.

14. Calvin, *Institutes*, I.xvii.6.

15. This is a common Mormon phrase that you can find, among other places, at www.lds.org.

16. Church leader Bruce McConkie, quoted in Millet, *A Different Jesus*, 20.

17. As quoted in Millet, *A Different Jesus*, 80.

18. See Lee Strobel, *The Case for the Real Jesus* (Grand Rapids: Zondervan, 2007), 157–87.

19. Rob Bell, *Velvet Elvis* (Grand Rapids: Zondervan, 2006), 17.

20. J. Gresham Machen, *The Virgin Birth of Christ* (Cambridge, UK: Lutterworth, 1987), 3.

21. *The Commentary of Dr. Zacharias Ursinus*, trans. G. W. Williard, 231.

22. Ibid., 215.

23. Quoted by J. I. Packer in *In My Place Condemned He Stood: Celebrating the Glory of the Atonement* (Wheaton: Crossway, 2008), 129. Packer himself warns against cheapening the atonement by making its application universal. "It comes about this way. We want to magnify the saving grace of God and the saving power of Jesus Christ. So we declare that God's redeeming love extends to every man, and that Christ has died to save every man. . . . And then, in order to avoid universalism, we have to depreciate all that we were previously extolling, and to explain that, after all, nothing that God and Christ have done can save us unless we add something to it; the decisive factor which actually saves us is our own believing. . . . This is a hollow anticlimax" (128–29).

24. Calvin, *Institutes*, 2.16.11.

25. J. Gresham Machen, *Christianity and Liberalism* (Grand Rapids: Eerdmans, 1923), 42.

26. As quoted in John Piper, *Contending for Our All* (Wheaton: Crossway, 2006), 116.

27. G. K. Chesterton, *Orthodoxy* (Chicago: Moody, 2009), 115.

28. Andrew Delbanco and Thomas Delbanco, "A.A. at the Crossroads," *The New Yorker*, 20 March 1995, accessed at http://www.aa-nia-dist11.or/Documents/cross.pdf.

29. There may be even earlier evidence. Polycarp, the famous martyr and Bishop of Smyrna, said that for eighty-six years he had served his King and Savior. In other words, Polycarp saw his whole life (ca. 69–ca. 155) as one of continuous allegiance to Christ. This may be an allusion to the baptism he received as an infant, marking him out as belonging to God.

30. See Wayne Grudem, *Systematic Theology* (Grand Rapids: Zondervan, 1994), 989–91.

31. The *Canons of Trent*, 22.2, declares: "And forasmuch as in this divine sacrifice which is celebrated in the mass, that same Christ is contained and immolated in an unbloody manner who once offered himself in a bloody manner on the altar of the cross; the holy Synod teaches that this sacrifice is truly propitiatory, and that by means thereof this is effected, that we obtain mercy and find grace. . . . For the victim is one and the same, the same now offering by the ministry of priests, who then offered himself on the cross, the manner alone of offering being different."

32. Interestingly, my edition of Ursinus's *Commentary* (an 1852 reprint) contains an introductory essay by John Williamson Nevin. At one point there is a footnote explaining that Nevin's critical remarks of questions 44 and 80 have been removed because the publication committee found them erroneous (xvii).

33. The Christian Reformed Church recently added this footnote to Q/A 80. "In response to a mandate from Synod 1998, the Christian Reformed Church's Interchurch Relations Committee conducted a study of Q. and A. 80 and the Roman Catholic Mass. Based on this study, Synod 2004 declared that 'Q. and A. 80 can no longer be held in its current form as part of our confession.' Synod 2006 directed that Q. and A. 80 remain in the CRC's text of the Heidelberg Catechism but that the last three paragraphs be placed in brackets to indicate that they do not accurately reflect the official teaching and practice of today's Roman Catholic Church and are no longer confessionally binding on members of the CRC." For more information see the 2008 Acts and Agenda for Synod (http://www.crcna.org/pages/syn odical.cfm). I am grateful to Lyle Bierma (Calvin), David Wells (Gordon-Conwell), Gregg

Allison (Southern), Mark Dever (Capitol Hill Baptist), and Scott Hahn (Franciscan University) for interacting with me on this point about the Mass, though I'm sure they don't all agree with what I've written in this chapter!

34. A monstrance is the vessel used in Catholic services to display (demonstrate) the consecrated Eucharistic host. After the elements are transubstantiated, they are placed in the monstrance so they can be adored and reverenced as Christ Himself.

35. Scott and Kimberly Hahn, *Rome Sweet Home: Our Journey to Catholicism* (San Francisco: Ignatius Press, 1993), 142. Scott Hahn is a popular Catholic apologist who teaches at the Franciscan University of Steubenville (Ohio). In the book Scott and Kimberly tell their story of converting from conservative Presbyterianism to Roman Catholicism.

36. Peter Kreeft, *Catholic Christianity: A Complete Catechism of Christian Beliefs Based on the Catechism of the Catholic Church* (San Francisco: Ignatius Press, 2001), 329.

37. Again, Kreeft: "Christ on the Cross of Calvary 2000 years ago and Christ on the altar of your local Catholic church today are the *same person*," 327 (emphasis in original).

38. For an explanation of why Ursinus in the original Catechism uses the word "unchaste" rather than explicity mention homosexuality, see the discussion in the appendix, "Does the Heidelberg Catechism Forbid Homosexual Behavior?"

39. Edwards's sermon "A Divine and Supernatural Light," in *The Sermons of Jonathan Edwards*, ed. Wilson H. Kimnack, Kenneth P. Minkema, and Douglas A. Sweeney (New Haven, Conn.: Yale Univ. Press, 1999), 127.

40. It is unclear to me whether the Heidelberg Catechism meant to forbid every artistic rendering of Jesus. On the one hand, Ursinus defends pictures or sculptures of historical scenes used outside the church (*Commentary*, 527). I would argue that depicting scenes from the Gospels paints a historical scene. On the other hand, Ursinus does not want God represented in any visible way (*Commentary*, 527–28). I'm not sure from his commentary if pictures of Christ count as history or as representing God. My guess is the latter more than the former. Thus, I may not be stating my "caution" against pictures of Jesus as strongly as Ursinus would want me to.

41. John Calvin, *Institutes* II.viii.22.

42. Jochem Douma, *Ten Commandments:* trans. Nelson D. Kloosterman (Philipsburg, N.J.: Presbyterian & Reformed Publishing, 1996), 90.

43. Quoted in *From Sabbath to Lord's Day*, ed. D. A. Carson (Eugene, Oreg.: Wipf and Stock, 1999), 314.

44. Calvin, *Institutes*. II.viii.28. Similarly, Calvin writes, "But there is no doubt that by the Lord Christ's coming the ceremonial part of this commandment was abolished. For He Himself is the truth, with whose presence all figures vanish; He is the body, at whose appearance the shadows are left behind. He is, I say, the true fulfillment of the Sabbath" (II.viii.31). For Calvin, observance of the Lord's Day was not a rigid affair but a matter of wisdom. "But I reply that we transcend Judaism in observing this day because we are far different from the Jews in this respect. For we are not celebrating it as a ceremony with the most rigid scrupulousness, supposing a spiritual mystery to be figured thereby. Rather, we are using it as a remedy needed to keep order in the church" (II.viii.33).

45. Calvin, *Institutes*, II.viii.36.

46. I am using the example of a man talking to his potential future father-in-law because this is common. But the situation could be a woman talking to her father or a son talking to his future mother-in-law or any other parent-child scenario when marriage is being considered. Since someone's parent is involved in every scenario, the issues are the same.

47. *The Teaching of the Twelve Apostles, Commonly Called the Didache*; accessed at http://www. ccel.org/ccel/richardson/fathers/Page_172.html.

48. John Calvin, *Harmony of the Law* (Ex. 21:22), vol. 3; accessed at http://www.ccel.org/ccel/ calvin/calcom05.ii.ii.v.ii.html.

49. Jason Byasse, "Not Your Father's Pornography," *First Things* 179 (2008): 15–18.

50. Ibid.

51. See John Piper, *Future Grace* (Sisters, Oreg.: Multnomah, 1998), 329–40.

52. As cited in Michael S. Horton, *The Law of Perfect Freedom* (Chicago: Moody, 1993), 222.

53. Ibid., 206.

54. Calvin, *Institutes* III.xx.42.

55. George Eldon Ladd, *A Theology of the New Testament* (Grand Rapids: Eerdmans, 1993), 103–17.

56. Ibid.

57. The content of the first two paragraphs and some of the wording come from Kevin DeYoung, *Just Do Something: A Liberating Approach to Finding God's Will* (Chicago: Moody, 2009).

58. http://www.robertgagnon.net/PittsburghPresbyteryOvertures.htm.

59. *Commentary of Dr. Zacharias Ursinus*, trans. G. W. Williard, 592.

60. Ibid., 591.

Acknowledgments

*I*n addition to thanking Zacharias Ursinus for writing most of the Heidelberg Catechism (I'll have to tell him in person later), I'd like to thank Dave DeWit and the gang at Moody; Andrew Wolgemuth, my fearless agent and (mostly) unashamed Royals fan; my parents for giving me my first copy of the Heidelberg Catechism; my administrative assistant, Jenny Olson, for helping with edits and taking good care of me; my childhood pastor, Steve VanderMolen, for making me read through all fifty-two Lord's Days; and my generous church family at University Reformed Church.

I also thank my denomination, the Reformed Church in America. The RCA and I aren't always on the same page, but it was in the RCA that I found the Heidelberg Catechism, and more importantly, it was in the RCA that Christ found me. I will always be grateful for those two finds.

And of course, my wife is as sweet and supportive as ever. Thanks, honey, for being my helpmate.

JUST DO SOMETHING

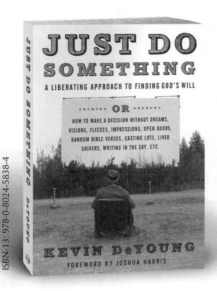

Hyperspiritual approaches to finding God's will just don't work. It's time to try something new: give up. Pastor and author Kevin DeYoung counsels Christians to settle down, make choices, and do the hard work of seeing those choices through. Too often, he writes, God's people jump from church to church, workplace to workplace, relational circle to relational circle, worrying that they haven't found God's perfect will for their lives. But God doesn't need to tell us what to do at each fork in the road. He's already revealed His plan for our lives: to love Him with our whole hearts, to obey His Word, and after that, to do what we like. No need for hocus-pocus. No reason to be directionally challenged. *Just do something.*

MOODY
PUBLISHERS

MoodyPublishers.com

WHY WE'RE NOT EMERGENT

Christianity Today Book of the Year Winner in 2009

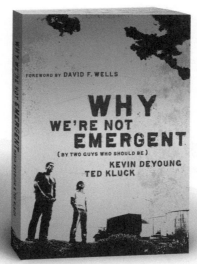

ISBN-13: 978-0-8024-5834-6

"You can be young, passionate about Jesus Christ, surrounded by diversity, engaged in a postmodern world, reared in evangelicalism and not be an emergent Christian. In fact, I want to argue that it would be better if you weren't." The emergent church is a strong voice in today's Christian community. And they're talking about good things: caring for the poor, peace for all men, loving Jesus. They're doing church a new way, not content to fit the mold. Again, all good. But there's more to the movement than that. Much more. Kevin and Ted are two guys who, demographically, should be all over this movement. But they're not. And *Why We're Not Emergent* gives you the solid reasons why. From both a theological and an on-the-street perspective, Kevin and Ted diagnose the emerging church. They pull apart interviews, articles, books, and blogs, helping you see for yourself what it's all about.

MOODY
PUBLISHERS

MoodyPublishers.com

WHY WE LOVE THE CHURCH

Christianity Today Book of the Year Winner in 2010

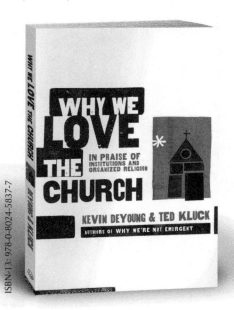

Authors Kevin DeYoung and Ted Kluck present the case for loving the local church. Their newest book paints a picture of the local church in all its biblical and real life guts, gaffes, and glory in an effort to edify local congregations and entice the disaffected back to the fold. It provides a solid biblical mandate to love and be part of the body of Christ and counteract the "leave church" books that trumpet rebellion and individual felt needs.

MOODY
PUBLISHERS

MoodyPublishers.com